Haunting Encounters

Haunting Encounters

The Ethics of Reading across Boundaries of Difference

Joanne Lipson Freed

Cornell University Press

Ithaca and London

First published 2017 by Cornell University Press

Printed in the United States of America

Library of Congress Cataloging-in-Publication Data
Names: Freed, Joanne Lipson, 1983– author.
Title: Haunting encounters : the ethics of reading across boundaries of
  difference / Joanne Lipson Freed.
Description: Ithaca : Cornell University Press, 2017. | Includes
  bibliographical references and index.
Identifiers: LCCN 2017013435 (print) | LCCN 2017018722 (ebook) |
  ISBN 9781501713828 (pdf) | ISBN 9781501713835 (ret) | ISBN
  9781501713767 | ISBN 9781501713767 (cloth : alk. paper)
Subjects: LCSH: Ghosts in literature. | Supernatural in literature. |
  Psychic trauma in literature. | Memory in literature. | Difference
  (Philosophy) in literature. | Transnationalism in literature. | Ghost
  stories—History and criticism. | American fiction—20th century—
  History and criticism. | American fiction—21st century—History
  and criticism. | Commonwealth fiction (English)—20th century—
  History and criticism. | Commonwealth fiction (English)—21st
  century—History and criticism.
Classification: LCC PS374.G45 (ebook) | LCC PS374.G45 F74 2017
  (print) | DDC 813/.0873309—dc23
LC record available at https://lccn.loc.gov/2017013435

Cornell University Press strives to use environmentally responsible
suppliers and materials to the fullest extent possible in the publishing
of its books. Such materials include vegetable-based, low-VOC inks
and acid-free papers that are recycled, totally chlorine-free, or partly
composed of nonwood fibers. For further information, visit our website
at cornellpress.cornell.edu.

For James and Nora

Contents

Acknowledgments

There are many, many people to thank for helping to bring this book into being. As someone who now teaches, I'll start by thanking my teachers. The faculty at Sidwell Friends School taught me to be curious, confident, and resilient, and my professors and classmates at Swarthmore College inspired me to consider the ways that literature might matter, ethically and politically, and always held my readings, and their own, to scrupulous account.

I am especially grateful to those at the University of Michigan who together enabled this project to take shape: Josh Miller, Jennifer Wenzel, Michael Awkward, and Amy Sara Carroll. In addition, the organizers of the Preparing Future Faculty program and the Center for Research on Learning and Teaching at the University of Michigan showed me how to be a practicing teacher-scholar who writes every day; without them, this book would likely never have been finished.

I owe many thanks to the participants and organizers of the 2014 Project Narrative Summer Institute at the Ohio State University, who helped me discover that, at heart, I've long been a narrative theorist. Robyn Warhol, in particular, has been an incredibly generous and inspiring mentor; she, along with my many PNSI friends, has welcomed me into a vibrant and nourishing intellectual community, of which I am grateful to be a part.

Early versions of some of these chapters have appeared previously in print, and the anonymous readers of those articles lent focus and acuity to several key readings throughout this book. Chapter 2 was first published, in somewhat different form, in *Comparative Literature Studies* 48.2, and is reprinted here with the journal's permission; similarly, chapter 3 appeared in *ARIEL* 43.2. I am also especially indebted to the three anonymous readers of this manuscript who, at various stages of the project's evolution, helped me to see its limitations clearly and pushed me to realize its promise. I am grateful to Helen Tartar for her early interest in this project, which gave me the confidence to move forward. And I could not have asked for a more engaged and supportive editor than Mahinder Kingra, who has been a tremendous advocate throughout the process of bringing this book, in its current form, into being.

Several of my colleagues at Oakland University, including Bailey McDaniel, Andrea Knutson, and Jeff Insko, were kind enough to read and respond to chapters of this book—in some cases, multiple times. Jeff Insko, in particular, was both a cheerleader and a stickler, as the situation warranted; I am especially grateful to him for pushing me to discover a scholarly voice that is authentically my own. The University Research Committee at Oakland provided important financial support in the form of a 2014 Faculty Research Grant. And I am tremendously grateful to Alison Powell, Alex Zamalin, and the fierce and fabulous members of the Junior Lady Club, who provided joyful encouragement and invaluable moral support during all the highs and lows of the last few years.

As the author of a book about reading across boundaries of difference, I am indebted to all my students at the University of Michigan, Ohio University, and Oakland University, who have intrepidly set out to do just that. My experiences in the classroom not only inform the claims throughout this book, but also, more importantly, motivate the most fundamental questions it aims to address. To all the students I have had the privilege of teaching, who enroll in English classes when STEM or preprofessional majors might seem more expedient and who work hard to make works of literature meaningful, this book is for, about, and inspired by you.

Last but not least, the Lipson, Freed, and Rowe families followed with loving concern the long, arduous, and often opaque process of writing a dissertation and turning it into a book. Particular thanks are due to Marcia Lipson, an indefatigable copy editor, without whom the writing in this book would be immeasurably less clear, precise, and readerly.

Most of all, to James Freed, a true partner in every sense of the word, I give my deepest and most loving gratitude.

Haunting Encounters

Introduction

FICTIONAL ENCOUNTERS

In Mahasweta Devi's novella "Pterodactyl, Puran Sahay, and Pirtha," the educated, progressive journalist Puran visits a famine-ravaged tribal village where he confronts something impossible: a dinosaur alive in contemporary India. Puran's encounter shocks him and forces him to reevaluate many of his assumptions about himself, his relationships, and his politics. Paradoxically, the creature, which is impossibly alien and mind-blowingly strange, appears in the most intimate of spaces—Puran discovers it in the hut where he is sleeping—and Puran feels an intense personal responsibility to care for it that is amplified, rather than diminished, by his recognition that he will never understand it. Puran's encounter with the pterodactyl fundamentally changes his relationship to the people of Pirtha, with whom he has little in common; instead of an observer, he becomes, at least provisionally, a participant in the communal life of the village. And after the pterodactyl's death, even though he recognizes that there is no way to report on what he has witnessed without subjecting the vulnerable tribal community to a media frenzy, he returns to his life and his work transformed.

Puran's experience captures the fundamental challenge of cross-cultural reading, especially when comparatively privileged readers attempt to engage with fiction from the margins: How can we respond ethically to stories that arrest us with their difference? How do we balance the feelings of closeness and intimacy that well-told stories inspire with an awareness that such acts of reading are marked by persistent differences in power? Devi's novella makes its way to the majority of Western academic readers in a form mediated by Gayatri Spivak's prominent role as the work's promoter, translator, and principal theorist, and her reading of "Pterodactyl" offers one compelling framework for responding to the difference it embodies. To Spivak, Puran's encounter with the pterodactyl exemplifies the model of ethical relation embodied in poststructuralist theory: *singularity*. Following this model, the possibility of entering into an ethical relationship with another (a person, a pterodactyl) relies first and foremost on the recognition of that other's absolute difference. The understanding of ethical singularity that Spivak applies to Devi's text offers a compelling framework for thinking about ethics in an era of globalization: because it emphasizes difference, rather than denying or seeking to transcend it, poststructuralist ethics suggests that our ability to form relationships with others might be as broadly inclusive as the diverse and increasingly interconnected world we inhabit.

As appealing as such an approach might seem, however, I also recall the hesitation and discomfort I first felt upon reading Devi's story, in which the valorization of "difference" seemed to veer perilously close to the dehumanizing gestures of colonialism, rendering the other irrational, inscrutable, primitive, and anachronistic—even destined for extinction! Was this allegory of the encounter with the other a story that I, a white, Western, academic reader, could inhabit in any ethical way?

The scant reassurance provided by Spivak's theoretical maneuvers, characteristically careful to mark both her own location and that of her readers, is further diminished by Devi's own postscript, which emphasizes that the figure of the pterodactyl was not derived directly from any particular tribal culture or belief system; rather, Devi explains, she has "deliberately conflated the ways, rules, and customs of different Austric tribes" in order "to express [her] estimation, derived of experience, of Indian tribal society."[1] Where was I to stand in relation to such an admittedly fictionalized and strategic representation of tribal culture, created by someone who was herself an outsider to the culture she depicts? This question might well seem to smack of a certain kind of entitlement: I am not the primary audience of the novella, and the potential discomfort of majoritarian readers like myself is hardly the most pressing concern for a writer such as Devi. But the alternative, from my perspective, is not reading, thinking, or caring about a text like "Pterodactyl" and dodging the responsibilities I might incur by reading a work such as this one, which in fundamental ways decenters my privileged reading position. Like Puran, who knows he must attempt to feed the pterodactyl even if his efforts are unlikely to succeed, because not trying would be unconscionable, the majoritarian readers of minority and Third World fiction have a responsibility to read—and endeavor to read ethically—precisely those texts that leave them uncertain where to stand.

Rather than opting out, disengaging from the ethical and imaginative claims of fictions that unsettle us with their difference, what does it look like to opt in? That is, in essence, the question this book seeks to answer. In an increasingly interconnected world, shaped by persistent inequalities and asymmetries of power, what role, if any, can literature play in bringing us into ethical relation with one another? How do we approach those works that challenge us with paradoxical demands to both recognize difference and forge meaningful connections across it? How do we respond to the residues of power that inhere in these textual encounters? And on what basis—if any—can we argue that reading literature from cultures or countries other than our own makes us better world citizens? In the chapters that follow, I focus on a particular subset of contemporary ethnic and Third World fiction that consciously addresses itself, at least in part, to privileged outsiders (frequently white and/or Western) across boundaries of cultural difference. In important ways, these works complicate familiar models of narrative ethics, both those that credit fiction with a special ability to inspire empathy and fellow feeling, and conversely, those, like Spivak's, that cite alterity, or difference, as the necessary foundation for ethical relationships.

Haunting is a recurring theme in these works and is an apt way of describing the possibilities and dangers involved in staging cross-cultural encounters in and through fiction. In some cases, the hauntings these works depict involve literal, embodied spirits, like the baby ghost who inhabits the house at 124 Bluestone Road in Toni Morrison's *Beloved*, or the ghost of Kari Saipu in Arundhati Roy's *The God of Small Things*, who roams the grounds of his former estate, pleading for a cigar. At other times, haunting is more metaphorical, as when victims of disappearance haunt the societies from which they have been violently erased, or past dreams haunt the disillusioned as they try to imagine a different future. In all these instances, however, haunting is a form of uncanny contact that troubles the boundaries between past and present, here and elsewhere, real and unreal, familiar and strange. The productive tension between sameness and difference that characterizes these works may resonate, to varying degrees, with other familiar accounts of psychic, ontological, or cultural haunting: a Freudian conception of the alien within the self,[2] Derrida's account of ghosts that hail us,[3] or the forms of cultural transmission or social erasure that are of central concern to Kathleen Brogan and Avery Gordon, respectively.[4] My central concern, in what follows, is with the way haunting manifests itself in the dynamic interactions between works of fiction and their readers at a distance. The uneasy juxtaposition of opposites that resist being reconciled or stabilized is, I contend, the essence of haunting's narrative and ethical force.

The hauntings depicted in these works—intense, temporary, and transformative encounters across difference—explicitly thematize the reading practices that the texts themselves invite. For readers who are cultural outsiders, the immersive experience of reading may indeed feel like a supernatural collapsing of time and space that delivers them into an unfamiliar world. On the one hand, therefore, these haunted fictions facilitate forms of contact that are impossible or improbable in reality, transporting American college students to the villages of tribal India or bringing contemporary readers into contact with recently emancipated slaves. The greater the distance traversed, however, the greater the risks: as these works suggest, hauntings are perilous; if carried too far, they can leave one unmoored, detached from the responsibilities of the here and now. As a result, these works stage not only hauntings, but also exorcisms, for both their characters and their readers. By repeatedly and intentionally disrupting the mimetic illusion that draws readers in, haunted fiction invites a reading practice that recognizes not only the limits of one's ability to know another, but also the limits of the fictional form to traverse distances of time and space that are also, inevitably, differences in power. Responding in concrete ways to the asymmetries that define their circulation and consumption, works of haunted fiction enact a particular form of narrative ethics that responds to both the demands and the risks of cross-cultural reading in a global age.

From the Politics of Representation to the Ethics of Reading

In order to talk meaningfully about the ethical implications of works that cross national and cultural boundaries, we first need a language for describing readers' relationships with literary texts. This claim might seem obvious; however, the dominant strains of both ethnic and postcolonial criticism have often skirted both the language of ethics and, by extension, the questions about readers that it seems logically to entail. Instead, the questions that have animated these fields largely concern the so-called politics of representation: how minority or Third World subjects are represented and by whom.[5] Are the depictions of specific characters and settings accurate and authentic, and do they serve to redress stereotypes or historical omissions? Who has the right to represent the subaltern subject, and what obligations are incurred in doing so? What ideologies have motivated and shaped these acts of representation, and when and how do they fall short? As valuable as such questions are, and as rich and varied the scholarship they have inspired, they risk disassociating "representations" from the acts of reading that render them meaningful. After all, the critique of representation derives its force from the fact that literary texts are created and, more importantly, read by real people. It's hard to imagine what harm even the most inaccurate, exploitative, or pernicious novel could do if it remained locked forever in a desk drawer. And the commitment to bringing minor sites and subjects into visibility, which motivates writers and critics alike, rests on the assumption that someone is doing the seeing and that their seeing matters.

Although a concern about readers and their responses to literary texts often remains implicit in ethnic and postcolonial studies scholarship, narrative theory takes up such questions directly, and despite a long-standing divide, these fields have more points of productive similarity in their methods and investments than either has generally acknowledged. Through its unapologetic commitment to social and ideological change as the project of both fiction writing and literary criticism, and the self-awareness about questions of positionality it demands, ethnic and postcolonial studies scholarship acknowledges, at least tacitly, that literary texts become meaningful by being read. For certain scholars, moreover, an alertness to questions of form in works of ethnic and Third World literature leads, as it does here, to an accounting of literary texts as dynamic meaning-making systems, yielding acute and persuasive accounts of how fiction perpetuates or challenges existing structures of power. Nevertheless, an explicit interest in how readers encounter works of fiction from the margins, and with what consequences, is often still enough to get the aspiring postcolonialist or ethnic studies scholar sent down the hall to some department in the social sciences, or perhaps even the School of Education. Claiming to examine questions of readership in and through the analysis of literary form, rather than survey data or ethnography, in turn, entails a methodological allegiance that because of its structuralist roots, has been dismissed by many ethnic and postcolonial studies scholars as falsely universalizing, unhistoricist, and apolitical.[6] Granting the commonsense assertion that readers are often the implicit subjects of the urgent questions about authenticity, appropriation, and resistance posed by ethnic and postcolonial studies, however, places one firmly in the terrain of narrative ethics—and, more broadly, rhetorical narrative theory.

Built on the recognition that all narrative, including fictional narrative, is an act of communication between teller and audience, rhetorical narrative theory directs our attention to the fundamental properties of a work's form and structure—including those that shape the reader's relationship to the depicted world—as the site and the source of a text's ethics. Moving forward from this premise, it's helpful to distinguish the different levels on which narrative can invoke ethical questions. Many of us are familiar with the kind of reading that seeks to diagnose and adjudicate the ethical dilemmas of characters within a fictional world—what James Phelan terms "the ethics of the told."[7] When we ask ourselves, or our students, if Tayo, Leslie Marmon Silko's protagonist in *Ceremony*, is right not to intervene as his friend Harley is tortured and killed, we are concerned with the ethics of the told. Like *Ceremony*, the other works of haunted fiction I consider certainly raise ethical questions on the level of the told: they depict characters who endeavor to forge connections with others and must grapple with the imperfect and provisional relationships that result. On this level, then, works of haunted fiction potentially exemplify ethical relationships across difference.

But narrative ethics also operates in these works on the level of reading and reception. Following Phelan, then, we might ask: "What, if any, are the ethical obligations of the audience to the narrative itself, to its materials, and to its author? What, if any, are the consequences of an audience's success or failure in meeting those obligations?" And perhaps most fundamentally, "Does reading narrative help one become a better, more ethically sound, person?"[8] This last question is relevant to all of us who, as scholars and teachers of literature, must justify the value of our daily reading and writing to ourselves, our academic institutions, and the public; but it is particularly so to those of us engaged in the study of ethnic and postcolonial literature, who see a clear and consequential link between the literature we study and the conditions of injustice that exist in the wider world. On what basis, then, can we claim that the act of reading fiction is not only pleasurable, but also morally improving, or that it might also help us live more ethically in our increasingly interconnected world?

One popular response to this question identifies empathy as literature's special province and the source of its improving powers.[9] The philosopher Martha Nussbaum is perhaps the most well-known proponent of the position that empathizing with fictional characters can cultivate readers' moral sensibilities, and thus lead them to act more justly toward others in the wider world. She argues that citizenship in a liberal democracy requires "the ability to think what it might be like to be in the shoes of a person different from oneself, to be an intelligent reader of that person's story, and to understand the emotions and wishes and desires that someone so placed might have."[10] Literature, so this logic goes, teaches readers to empathize with others in ways that translate beyond the realm of fiction and into civic life, by making us better, more "intelligent reader[s]" of others' stories. There are, however, good reasons to be skeptical of claims such as Nussbaum's, which identify empathy as the source of literature's ethical significance. For one, even if we grant that literature is uniquely adept at eliciting empathy from its readers, there's little empirical evidence to justify the link that Nussbaum and others posit between narrative empathy and prosocial action. An additional concern, I will suggest, has to do with the logic of sameness on which empathy relies, which fundamentally limits its ethical force.

While it might make intuitive sense that empathizing with fictional characters predisposes readers to empathize more readily with nonfictional people, a growing body of interdisciplinary scholarship casts doubt on this assumption. Most notably, Suzanne Keen's recent study, *Empathy and the Novel*, investigates and ultimately fails to establish a factual basis for claims about the larger social ramifications of narrative empathy. While Keen agrees that empathizing with literary characters is an essential and often enjoyable aspect of reading fiction, her careful review of research studies reveals no clear link between reading fiction and feeling empathy for real-world others or for taking concrete action on those others' behalf.[11] Indeed, she suggests that the very unreality of fiction might facilitate empathetic engagement by providing readers with a safe space in which to suspend their natural impulses toward doubt and suspicion.[12] Complementing Keen's findings, a recent study by Angus Fletcher and John Monterosso suggests that certain literary devices, such as free indirect discourse, might encourage readers to exercise imaginative restraint, rather than the kind of extension that empathy calls for.[13] Crucially, the claim that readers of fiction empathize more readily, and thus treat others more justly, requires that empathetic feelings be generalized beyond the specific textual situation that inspires them; there is little empirical evidence, however, to suggest that is the case.

In addition to studies such as Keen's, which call this kind of generalizing move into question, there is another more fundamental problem with claiming empathy as a driver of narrative ethics, or ethics in general: its reliance on the logic of sameness. In contemporary usage, empathy, the ability to "feel with" another, is distinguished from sympathy, or "feeling for," as a state in which one's emotions mirror those attributed to the other.[14] (By contrast, pity, a feeling typically associated with sympathy, is not an emotion one would ascribe to the person being pitied.) But this kind of "feeling with" relies on at least some degree of perceived similarity, some basis for fellow feeling: as Ray Sorensen puts it, "stepping into the other guy's shoes works best when you resemble him."[15] The less one has in common with another, the more difficult it becomes to empathize, and the greater the risk of making false or inappropriate assumptions based on one's own experience. As a basis for ethical action, therefore, empathy is most attenuated where it is arguably most necessary: in our interactions with those we define as other. And if empathy provides at best a dubious foundation for narrative ethics in general, it is even more problematic as a justification for the ethical value of cross-cultural reading, which we hope will bridge the divide between disparate people and societies.

An alternative model, rooted in poststructuralist theory, identifies difference, rather than sameness, as the source of literature's ethical force in a globalizing word. What literature teaches us, in this model, are the limits of our ability to know another, and the attitude we cultivate through reading is the circumspection that such a recognition demands. In contrast to empathy's basis in sameness, the "difference model" of narrative ethics is grounded in the concept of singularity: the absolute difference that separates oneself from any other person and, in doing so, makes one singularly responsible to that other.[16] Rather than seeking to know the other, ethical singularity demands that one meet the other, in the language of philosopher Emmanuel Levinas, face to face; this encounter is both the site and the source of ethical responsibility that is derived from, rather than diminished by, alterity.[17] This understanding of narrative ethics offers an alternative way of thinking about how literature—and in particular, the interaction between text and reader—might become ethically significant. In contrast to the empathy model, which suggests that literature cultivates a sense of sameness and shared humanity in its readers, the difference model argues that literature stages encounters with otherness that lay the groundwork for ethical responsibility.

Privileging this latter model, the literary scholars that Dorothy Hale terms the "new ethicists" identify difference as a fundamental feature of the novel's aesthetic.[18] On the level of character and plot, literary texts force their readers to confront the unknowability of others' minds; Hale cites, for instance, the moment in Henry James's *Washington Square* when Catherine Sloper inexplicably rejects her suitor as "an experience of the other that surprises us in its intractability, its refusal to conform to what we imagine we know."[19] We cannot discern Catherine's motives, and James does not deliver them to us; rather than judging her, therefore, we can only " 'care' for her as other."[20] It is not only characters, however, whom readers must encounter as other; it is also the literary text itself. Simply put, a work of fiction is like reality, but not quite of it, and the otherness that separates the fictional and nonfictional worlds, making storyworld truths unverifiable, can itself inspire ethical engagement. As Adam Newton puts it, "one faces a text as one might face a person, having to confront the claims raised by that very immediacy, an immediacy of contact, not of meaning."[21] Following such a model, the very fictionality of fiction gives rise to the conditions in which ethics become possible; it is, as Newton suggests, not merely a "laboratory" for studying ethics, but an enactment of ethics itself.[22]

By seeing in fictional form the very infrastructure of ethical relation, poststructuralist narrative ethics offers a different and more persuasive link between narrative structures and readers' ethical actions or attitudes in the wider world. In the empathy model, in order to generalize their feelings of empathy for characters beyond the pages of fiction, readers must see the fictional world and the nonfictional world as fundamentally contiguous. The alterity model, by contrast, requires no such assumption; instead, recognizing that literary texts are not real invites readers to interact with them—ethically—by recognizing their difference. Following the logic of singularity, it is because of this difference that we incur ethical responsibilities through the act of reading fiction.

This kind of poststructuralist narrative ethics seems particularly well suited to the task of cross-cultural reading, for several reasons. By suggesting that knowledge is antithetical to ethical engagement, such an understanding of literature avoids taking it as the source of anthropological information in ways that reduce the other to an object of study. A narrative ethics founded on alterity, moreover, thrives in situations where empathy might be overcome by the effect of alienation—where, for instance, differences in race, culture, or belief threaten to make a character's actions or attitudes incomprehensible to certain readers. Indeed, where narrative empathy fails to translate beyond the pages of fiction, the openness to difference that fiction reading cultivates would seem to provide an ideal mechanism for forging ethical relationships across national or cultural divides. The poststructuralist dictum that "every other is completely other" seems like wise counsel in such circumstances, where it promises both a basis for connecting across difference and a backstop against the colonizing imagination.

While it may be energized by the strength of such totalizing claims about difference, however, the project of cross-cultural reading, which requires us to grapple with types or degrees of otherness that are historically specific and materially consequential, also places them under strain. There's something perhaps a little bit too easy in the deconstructive move that equates intersubjective difference with social difference, flattening out history, politics, and power in the process. Consider the challenge of a novel like Toni Morrison's *Beloved*. Morrison's novel is replete with claims to know others that entail an exercise of power: from schoolteacher's book, to Sethe's absolute claim over her infant daughter's life, to the black community's conviction that Sethe's mother-love is "too thick."[23] Demonstrating—at times dramatically—the interpersonal and psychic costs of such claims, *Beloved* makes a powerful argument for engaging with others across difference and abandoning the claim to know. This is the spirit in which the black women of Cincinnati ultimately gather, despite fundamental differences in their values, perspectives, and beliefs, to exorcise the ghost haunting the house at 124 Bluestone Road and save the lives of Sethe and her surviving daughter, Denver. In a similar way, *Beloved* also challenges its readers to accommodate themselves to difference—in the form of Sethe's infanticidal mother-love, and in the form of the novel's own supernatural conceit.

In this sense, then, the ethical project of *Beloved* looks similar to that of *Washington Square*: by challenging readers to confront the unknowability of fictional others, it both models forms of ethical relation and reminds us of the necessary gap between fiction and reality. But Toni Morrison faces another kind of challenge that Henry James does not: the likelihood that a former slave like Sethe will be seen—by both characters and readers—as less than human. That is certainly Paul D.'s reaction: he learns of Sethe's infanticide and promptly "count[s] her feet," implying that her actions have reduced her to the level of an animal, then leaves her (198). If failing to recognize Sethe's difference is an act of domination, failing to recognize her sameness—her common humanity—removes her from the sphere of ethical relation entirely. This is simply not a risk in the same way for a wealthy white woman like James's Catherine Sloper. While her rejection of her suitor may baffle us, it will not cause us, as readers of the Western canon, to doubt her basic humanity, since there is no similar precedent for making such an assumption about a woman of Catherine's race and social status. Are we really to believe, then, that Catherine is as inscrutable to Henry James's readers as Sethe is to Toni Morrison's or that the ethical stakes of suspending our judgment of these two women and their actions are comparable?

This asymmetry in the forms of difference that James's and Morrison's fictions instantiate perfectly illustrates the risk of ideological mystification that Sue J. Kim attributes to what she terms "otherness postmodernism," a critical tendency that, she argues, paradoxically flattens out the very forms of difference it celebrates as inherently resistant.[24] Through its privileging of absolute alterity, Kim asserts, otherness postmodernism fails "to account for the mediations between sameness and difference—the messy in-betweens that constitute most actual social processes."[25] Concerns like the ones Kim articulates inspire an understandable impulse to qualify the totalizing claim that "tout autre est tout autre" (every other is completely other), in response to the particular ethical demands of cross-cultural reading.[26] Derek Attridge, for instance, exemplifies the ways that postcolonial theorists often temper the strong claim of alterity that poststructuralist narrative ethics voices. According to Attridge, literature requires its readers "to respect its otherness, to respond to its singularity, to avoid reducing it to the familiar and the utilitarian *even while attempting to understand it.*"[27] This seemingly small caveat—that respecting the text's otherness does not absolve one of the obligation to engage with it and attempt to make it meaningful—reflects the kind of concern I have outlined above: that readers might disengage from works they find too foreign and thus fail to see themselves as incurring any form of responsibility through their acts of reading. If the encounter between reader and text is analogous to the encounter with the other from which ethics emerges, formulations like Attridge's suggest that we cannot take the staging of that encounter for granted. If we are to enter into ethical relationships with distant others, it would seem, we must first bridge physical, cultural, and ideological divides to achieve some form of proximity.

As a mechanism for traversing such distances, fiction can seem almost magical; indeed, part of its appeal is the apparent ease with which it transcends the concrete material realities—like segregated schools and neighborhoods, or border checkpoints—that separate us from one another in real life. This effect is heightened by the mimetic illusion of realism, which seamlessly delivers us, to use David Palumbo-Liu's terminology, into a fictional world.[28] This aspect of fictional narrative is ideally suited to the task of establishing contact across difference, a task that, as I have suggested, is the necessary prerequisite to ethical singularity. At the same time, however, Attridge's emphasis on difficult reading—works whose formal experiments disrupt the immersive pleasures of mimesis—reveals an underlying suspicion that fiction might make access to the other too easy or that the literary sleight of hand by which it is accomplished might be too thoroughly concealed. If literature has the power to bring us into imaginative relationship with people of vastly different circumstances than our own, there must be some textual residue or marker of the distance that has been traveled and of the structures of power that make these two positions nonequivalent. Thus, although poststructuralist theory generates a persuasive account of how reading fiction becomes ethical, applying this model to the particular imperatives of cross-cultural reading requires certain caveats. If fiction is to inspire new and more ethical relationships across boundaries of difference, it must first allow readers to come into contact with others through the work of the literary imagination. But if it is to carry out such transit responsibly, it must not allow imagination to be mistaken for reality, for to do so would deny concrete and consequential differences in power.

Not surprisingly, then, many of the most persuasive recent accounts of so-called border-crossing fiction are concerned equally with the formal and thematic elements that inspire a sense of connection and with those that productively resist the easy assimilation of stories from the margins.[29] Shameem Black, for instance, examines the ways that writers of contemporary global fiction "attempt to engage significant otherness without inevitably trapping their objects of representation within the prisons of their own fantasies and fears," and she retains a fundamental optimism that such negotiations can be carried out successfully.[30] Similarly, Palumbo-Liu's account of literary texts as among the various delivery systems that bridge national, cultural, and even corporeal divides calls attention to the way that historically specific forms of difference place these systems of sameness under strain, but also identifies "redemptive moments" of connection made possible through the workings of literary aesthetics.[31]

In the works of fiction I consider, haunting is the exemplary figure for the more qualified form of contact across difference that scholars like Black, Palumbo-Liu, and Attridge each call for: intense and transient, but also potentially transformative. Like the encounter with a fictional other, which flouts the rules of time and space, the encounter with the ghost is supernatural, impossible yet captivating. And just as it is perilous to forget the distinction between the fictional and the real, the hauntings in these works are necessarily temporary states, from which characters must ultimately emerge. The literal and metaphorical hauntings these works depict not only illustrate the challenges of connecting across boundaries of difference, but also echo the powerful yet circumscribed relationships the texts themselves endeavor to construct with their own global readers. Neither transparent nor obscure, the formal strategies these works employ invite readers in, while at the same time insisting that our access to the fictional world is profoundly contingent and necessarily temporary. This is, in some ways, a weaker claim than poststructuralist narrative ethics in general would advance, but it is, I argue, one that better responds to the concrete historical conditions and specific structures of power that these works explicitly engage.

Haunted Texts, Haunted Reading

Haunting is a generative metaphor for the dynamic tension between sameness and difference that animates a wide range of ethnic and postcolonial fiction: the ghost is at once familiar and strange, present and absent, a figment of the past or the elsewhere intruding into the here and now. Like the young woman with lineless hands in *Beloved* or Devi's pterodactyl, ghosts appear in intimate spaces and captivate us with their difference in ways that are both enthralling and utterly unfathomable. Freud's concept of the uncanny—that which is eerily familiar by virtue of being repressed—is an archetypal example,[32] but the same productive tension between the intimate and the alien that Freud locates within the individual mind also characterizes the dynamics of social inclusion and marginalization, and the discourses and practices of knowledge production they shape. As sociologist Avery Gordon suggests, haunting deserves to be taken seriously as evidence of events or individuals pushed to society's margins, whose incomplete erasure troubles dominant narratives of history. "The ghost or the apparition," she writes, "is one form by which something lost, or barely visible, or seemingly not there to our supposedly well-trained eyes, makes itself known or apparent to us."[33]

By reminding us of history's exclusions, haunting also calls into question fundamental assumptions about the linear progression of time. Indeed, as Derrida's evocative coinage "hauntology" reminds us, haunting is an encounter with ontological difference that is also fundamentally an experience of temporal disjuncture.[34] For Derrida, this condition of time being "out of joint" (as it is for Hamlet, when he confronts his father's ghost) enables a kind of justice that, in a Levinasian sense, exceeds rational calculation or reciprocity.[35] Similarly, for John Su, the temporal doubling of being haunted is a necessary condition of ethical engagement. Also drawing on Levinas, Su suggests that the a priori quality of ethical responsibility means that individuals can recognize the ethical implications of their choices only in retrospect, by perceiving "a discrepancy between what *is* and what *could have been.*"[36] Characterizing ethics as an ongoing state of moral deliberation that can never be fully resolved, he cites Zygmunt Bauman's assertion that "the moral self is a self always haunted by the suspicion that it is not moral enough."[37]

In the works I consider here, haunting is depicted as just such a condition of ontological and temporal unsettlement, one that opens the possibility of new and more ethical kinds of relationships across difference. More than simply depicting hauntings, however, these works reproduce these dynamics for their readers, whose imaginative abilities are engaged by the very unknowability of the fictional world that leaves them uncertain of how to respond. Much like the untimeliness of haunting, which opens a space of possibility outside of or beyond rational decision making and calculated action, fiction reading disrupts the temporal progression of everyday life, inviting us to experience, at least temporarily, a similar state of ethical suspension. While a work of fiction may illustrate the ethical dilemmas that characters grapple with, its accounts of those dilemmas arrive to us belatedly, through the vehicle of narration, and readers' real-world responses to fiction's ethical appeals—engaging in dialogue, say, or joining a protest—can take place only when the act of reading has concluded. For this reason, therefore, narrative theory is an especially productive framework for tracing the ethical effects that arise in and through the process of reading. Building from the foundational premise that narrative is an account of sequential action that unfolds in time, narrative theory has developed a rich sensitivity to temporal progression on various narrative levels: the sequence of events that comprise the tale (*fabula*), the potentially distinct sequence of its telling (*sujet*), and how they interact to shape the reader's experience of the text. This alertness to narrative's dynamic emotional and ethical effects as they occur in and through time allows my account of haunted fiction to go beyond primarily thematic studies of haunted fiction, such as Kathleen Brogan's, as well as more conventionally formalist accounts of border-crossing fiction like Black's or Palumbo-Liu's, which are less closely attuned to this dimension of fictional meaning-making.

Indeed, in the chapters that follow, my arguments about the ethical implications of specific textual features often hinge on questions of progression: the ways in which a reader's interpretive inclinations and emotional allegiances are formed or transformed as he or she moves sequentially through the text. The accounts of political disappearance that I examine in chapter 3, for instance, leverage the untimely quality of fictional narration to cultivate their readers' loyalties for recognizable individuals who will subsequently become "the disappeared"—a temporal progression that reverses the typical human-rights narrative, in which a victim's violent erasure necessarily precedes his or her discursive recovery. And in chapter 4, it is the repetitive structure of both *Falling Man* and *The Beautyful Ones Are Not Yet Born* that allows readers to remain open to new interpretive possibilities that belie these works' apparent pessimism. Attending to the temporal unfolding of fictional narrative in this way allows me to

suspend, to a great degree, the impulse to sum up the often con-
flicting or contradictory elements of these works' appeals to their
readers (as, for instance, any notion of "redemptive moments"
would necessarily seem to do).[38] Rather than attempting to stabi-
lize these dynamics, an approach informed by rhetorical narrative
theory is better equipped to account for the ways in which works
of haunted fiction hold their readers in states of generative suspension. This kind of openness to radical uncertainty is tenable,
however, only when we recognize that fiction reading, like haunting, is a necessarily temporary state.

For an example, let's turn again to Puran and his encounter
with the pterodactyl, which I examine in greater detail in chapter 1. When Puran arrives in Pirtha to document the devastat-
ing famine there, he finds something astonishingly unexpected: a
dinosaur-like creature alive in present-day India. Coming face-to-
face with the pterodactyl demolishes Puran's attitude of sophisticated intellectual detachment: whereas previously he had sought
to investigate, understand, and document the social and economic
policies that oppress India's tribal minority, his connection to the
pterodactyl is immediate, visceral, and irrational. Despite his profound sense of obligation toward the creature, which he believes to
be an embodiment of the tribal past, Puran knows nothing about
its basic needs and can only guess at the significance of its intense,
inscrutable gaze. While the pterodactyl is alive, Puran immerses
himself in the life of the village, but he stays only long enough to
witness the creature's death and mourn its passing in accordance
with tribal customs. He understands implicitly that he cannot remain in Pirtha and that he can never speak of the supernatural
events he has witnessed; he returns to his former life, however,
transformed by this encounter. He continues to write about tribal
oppression in conventional, political terms, but never glibly, as

before, and in his personal life, he embraces the uncertainty inherent in building meaningful relationships with others.

Puran's encounter with the pterodactyl epitomizes the dynamics of haunting that appear, in some form, in each of the works I consider. In the world that Puran knows and believes himself to inhabit, a creature like the pterodactyl is an impossibility; yet, face-to-face with it, he can't deny its existence or explain it away. Its appearance is both symptomatic of the historical conditions that have made Indian tribals an oppressed and disenfranchised minority and also utterly inexplicable in such conventional terms. In a similar way, works of haunted fiction make visible what history has made invisible or unimaginable: suppressed pasts, experiences of trauma, and the subjectivities of those denied full personhood. As the pterodactyl's caretaker, Puran has no choice but to use his imagination to construe the creature's needs and draw on his own resources (including his own allotment of food in the famine-ravaged region) to satisfy them as best he can. To do otherwise—to watch the pterodactyl starve—would be unconscionable. Like Puran, these works' majoritarian readers incur a form of imaginative responsibility precisely by virtue of the distance that separates them from the depicted world; none of Devi's readers can know, in a conventional sense, what it is like to be a starving, illiterate tribal villager, any more than Puran can know what pterodactyls eat, but it is precisely because we cannot know that we have a responsibility to imagine.

In a more triumphalist narrative, perhaps, this effort would be sufficient and Puran would successfully nurse the pterodactyl back to health, but this is not the kind of story Devi offers us. The pterodactyl's death is inevitable, and it is because Puran cannot fathom its thoughts or desires, he believes, that he is obligated to witness its demise. Like Puran, whose efforts to save the pterodactyl must prove insufficient, English-language readers of the novella, in particular, are constantly reminded of imagination's limits, both by the story itself and by Spivak's intentionally demanding translation of the Bengali source text. Much as Puran undergoes an exorcism of sorts, participating in mourning rituals for the pterodactyl and then returning to his own everyday life, the novella concludes by pushing its readers away, underscoring its own contingent status as fiction with its short but unsettling author's note. For Puran, Devi makes clear, the sphere of ethical action lies beyond Pirtha, in his role as a father, a husband, and a journalist; although he cannot save the pterodactyl, his act of witnessing changes him, allowing him to make good on his responsibilities toward others in his life. In a similar way, Devi's text reminds her readers of the limits of the fictional encounter and directs us outward, where the new forms of feeling and imagination we may have discovered through reading can give rise to ethical action in the wider world.

Each of the works of haunted fiction I consider carries out a similar balancing act, drawing readers in but also marking the limits of their engagements with fictional worlds. The result is a rich interplay between mimesis and metafiction that simultaneously trades on and overtly interrogates literature's immersive power. Reading haunted fiction requires an act of imagination analogous to feeding the pterodactyl: when confronted by characters who differ from themselves, readers must draw on their own imaginations to fill in where knowledge fails. This is precisely the area in which realist representation excels, creating fictional worlds that draw readers in and compel them to imagine others, using their own emotions and experiences as raw materials. But haunted fiction also illustrates that imagination, if mistaken for either knowledge or experience, can do as much harm as good. Unlike traditional realism, which leaves its mimetic illusion unquestioned, haunted fiction invites readers, through a variety of means, to reflect on their acts of imagination, setting limits on the fictional encounter in ways that respond to the ethical demands of cross-cultural reading. As readers of haunted fiction, we must not only feed the pterodactyl, but do so with the knowledge of its inevitable death.

Ultimately, therefore, haunted fiction encourages its readers to interrogate the assumption that reading fiction, in and of itself, can be an ethically significant act. In particular, these works put pressure on the notion that we can "care for" a fictional character like Catherine or Sethe "as other," in the ethically charged sense that Hale describes.[39] Like the ghost whose most basic needs are impossible to satisfy, the characters we encounter in the pages of fiction are not the people we imagine them to be, but rather aesthetic constructs, fundamentally beyond the reach of our proffered concern or care. Recognizing this fact gives the lie to the quixotic idealism of those scholars, educators, and pundits who elevate "multicultural" or "global" fiction as a viable substitute for meaningful encounters across difference in the nonfictional world. I sincerely hope that my students grow, as I have grown, by reading about fictional characters who are different from themselves and cultivating an openness to others' thoughts and experiences. However, I want to resist the opportunistic elision that presents fiction reading as a cheap and easy alternative to real-world diversity and equality of access. Anticipating and resisting the risk of being appropriated in precisely this way, works of haunted fiction employ a variety of strategies that intentionally distance their readers from the storyworlds they depict, insisting on the perils of mistaking imagination for reality.

That is not to say, however, that imaginative encounters with works of fiction, like encounters with ghosts, are without material consequence. In Roy's *The God of Small Things*, which I address in chapter 2, Ammu awakens from a dream in which, in contrast to her bleak waking life, she was briefly happy. "Does that count?" her precocious twins ask her. "If you eat fish in a dream, does it count? Does it mean you've eaten fish?"[40] While the answer to this question seems fairly clear-cut in the case of eating fish, it is less so in the case of an emotion like happiness. Roy's narrator initially asserts, tautologically, that "only what *counts* counts," but then suggests that the content of the mind and the imagination can indeed be consequential in the material world (208). Ammu's mistaken certainty that she knows what life has in store for her, "because if in a dream you've eaten fish, it means you've eaten fish" (213), sets in motion a chain of events with life-altering and life-ending results. Acts of imagination can "count," Roy seems to suggest, at least inasmuch as they have concrete, real-world ramifications. But the patent implausibility of Ammu's formula, which equates dream fish and real fish, undermines any simple notion of their equivalency. Being happy in a dream may "count" for something, but only indirectly, just as eating fish in a dream cannot itself abate one's hunger. For Ammu, at least, the unreality of her dream yields a form of transformative imagination, awakening her to the possibility of romance with the low-caste carpenter, Velutha, to which the social strictures of her world had previously blinded her. The promise of haunted fiction is that for its readers, it might inspire a similar openness to unseen possibilities, unrecognized connections, and alternative futures.

To fully understand how works of fiction like "Pterodactyl," *The God of Small Things*, and the others I consider might give rise to forms of transformative imagination, I argue, we must attend to the particular ways in which these texts engage and position their readers through concrete, recognizable narrative strategies. A foundational conceit of this project is that literary texts both anticipate and shape the responses of their global readers in and through their formal and aesthetic practices. In the chapters that follow, therefore, I employ close reading, rather than methods like market analysis or reader-response criticism, to make sense of the ways in which works of haunted fiction cannily position their readers and subtly shape their imaginative and emotional responses to the stories they tell. Although attending closely to these textual structures cannot fully account for the varied and even idiosyncratic responses of these works' real readers, such an analysis allows us to recognize the complex maneuvers these texts carry out to manage the imaginative engagements of readers at a distance. And although the conditions of these works' global circulation and reception can and will continue to evolve, the fundamental features of their narrative form that determine readers' encounters with their imagined worlds—like the order in which events are narrated, or the perspective from which they are told—will not.

By acknowledging that works of fiction seek to carry out ethical work in and through the operation of literary form, moreover, I do not intend to suggest that particular forms are inherently tied to salutary ethical effects. To the contrary, following Caroline Levine, I want to recognize the plasticity and contextual specificity of forms and their affordances, which resist exclusive affiliations or deterministic outcomes.[41] The textual analysis I carry out in each of the following chapters calls attention to the way in which particular narrative elements shape the way readers interact with the depicted world and position themselves in relation to it. Although any literary text can generate a variety of possible responses, the conventionalized practices and expectations of readers interact with textual structures in ways that incentivize certain responses and disincentivize others.[42] Thus, readers of *Ceremony* who do not share Tayo's belief in an alternate narrative of American history can be encouraged to embrace it, at least provisionally, by their desire to see Tayo as a hero who is granted the happy ending that the novel has prepared us to expect, rather than as a coward who abandons a friend in his hour of need. Tracing such interactions reveals these texts to be more than passive objects of cross-cultural circulation and consumption. Quite the opposite: the narrative strategies these works employ make them surprisingly resilient (though not, of course, immune) to many of the types of appropriation or misreading to which they might be subjected as they traverse boundaries of culture and power in the Western literary mainstream.

Comparative Encounters

The works I consider here are intentionally diverse, drawn from South Asia, Latin America, and West Africa, as well as multiple ethnic traditions within the United States. The contemporary time period they represent is also broadly defined, beginning in the 1960s, in the aftermath of the civil rights and anticolonial movements, and continuing into the twenty-first century. These epochal political movements, which establish difference as a conceptual category with urgent ethical stakes, provide the necessary context for the questions these works pose and the negotiations they carry out. Nevertheless, it is often a frustration with politics that animates their formal and aesthetic interventions. Whereas politics, by its nature, privileges categories that are generalizable and principles that are actionable, ethics, by contrast, provides a framework for thinking about relationships across difference that may by their very definition lie outside of the realm of rational decision making. Indeed, as Black observes, "to talk about politics is often to reveal how literary forms reproduce political hierarchies and inequalities; to talk about ethics ... allows us to identify forms of fiction that may exceed such reproduction."[43] When Roy's Comrade Pillai fails to intercede on behalf of an Untouchable party-member, then makes political hay out of his murder; or when revolutionary nationalists and embezzling plutocrats in *The Beautyful Ones Are Not Yet Born* turn out to be one and the same; or when, in *Falling Man*, even the deaths of thousands fail to call the United States to account as "a power that interferes, that occupies," politics in these works comes to seem flawed and deeply suspect as a mechanism for acknowledging or traversing forms of difference.[44] Responding to a contemporary reality in which politics seems increasingly disarticulated from a more fundamental sense of right and wrong, these works appeal to their readers on other terms.

Among the many contemporary works that take difference as their central theme, the works of haunted fiction I consider here are distinguished by the degree to which they invite the engagements of readers at a distance—and in particular, the white, Western readers who are often the most powerful and visible members of that constituency. Some of these works have circulated more widely than others; for example, the lyrical prose of writers like Arundhati Roy and Michael Ondaatje has garnered major international prizes, and a syllabus-friendly novel like *Ceremony* is quickly pressed into the service of multicultural inclusion in U.S. college classrooms. But even works that have circulated less broadly, such as *The Beautyful Ones Are Not Yet Born*, Ayi Kwei Armah's bleak account of postindependence Ghana, or Gayatri Spivak's intentionally opaque English translations of Devi's writing, have traveled within the narrower context of the Western academy. Pushing back against the long-standing critical tendency, especially in postcolonial studies, to celebrate works for their aesthetic opacity or resistant particularity, I also want to recognize the value of those works, or those dimensions of works, that open themselves to imaginative engagement and interpretive circulation.[45]

In different ways, each of these works carries out the balancing act I have previously described: inviting their readers to enter into distant or unfamiliar fictional worlds, while carefully resisting the forms of appropriation that such an invitation might seem to authorize. For this reason, I include both an American feature film (*Missing*) and a novella originally written in Bengali ("Pterodactyl") in an archive comprised primarily of Anglophone novels. Despite differences in medium or language, both film and novella share the defining rhetorical structures and aesthetic investments of the other works in this study: they are concerned with imagining the lives of others and marking the limits of such imaginative acts. Similarly, the level of artistic refinement or high-cultural cachet attributed to the various works I consider has little bearing on the questions of narrative ethics that are of central concern throughout this study. Although certain of these works may be characterized as more popular (and thus, implicitly, less artful) than others, the rhetorical maneuvers they carry out, which anticipate and subtly shape the ways in which they are taken up by distant readers, are uniformly complex, sophisticated, and worthy of sustained analysis.

Placing these works side by side—staging yet another set of encounters across difference—I draw on the logic of haunting that the texts themselves provide. Like literary ghosts traversing temporal and geographic boundaries, comparative readings such as these have the potential to challenge the conventional configurations of literary fields and disciplines. In particular, the comparative encounters in these works, and the lessons about sameness and difference that emerge from them, have the potential to recast the long-standing and seemingly intractable debate about the study of world literature in potentially productive ways.[46] The pitched disciplinary stand-off between advocates of World Literature, on the one hand, and the practitioners of Comparative Literature, on the other, is animated by the same fundamental tension between sameness and difference that lies at the heart of each of the works of fiction included in this study. Do we privilege sameness, celebrating the ways that texts travel and accepting their invitations to engage imaginatively with people and places at a distance? Or do we privilege difference, emphasizing the ways that texts are linked to particular local contexts and thus require specific and demanding competencies to be interpreted appropriately? Even the most persuasive arguments from either camp—and there have been many—don't fundamentally reconfigure or resolve this defining tension because, in essence, both sides of the debate are correct. Haunted fiction, in responding to the particular imperatives of cross-cultural reading, underscores this fact, illustrating the ways in which both sameness and difference are essential to our ethical encounters with literary texts. It is a mistake to ignore, out of a spirit of scholarly purism, the ways that texts invite us to connect imaginatively with the people and places they depict. Even the least yielding fiction reaches out to its readers in this way and, in doing so, creates the possibility of ethical engagement. At the same time, however, it is by confronting the fictionality of fiction—its ontological difference, or noncontinuity with the reality its readers inhabit—that reading can inspire forms of meaningful ethical responsibility in the wider world.

In each of the following chapters, I examine a pair of works that illustrate, in different cultural and aesthetic contexts, how fiction becomes ethical through the operation of sameness and difference. Chapter 1 offers a foundational reading of two contemporary works in which literal, embodied ghosts or specters intrude into and transform the terrain of traditional literary realism: Toni Morrison's *Beloved* and Mahasweta Devi's novella "Pterodactyl, Puran Sahay, and Pirtha." Morrison's novel has been read so widely and to such acclaim that it's easy to take its central conceit for granted; placing it alongside Devi's much less well-known novella underscores the significance of both works' aesthetic and political interventions. Both works are engaged in the project of speaking for those at the margins of the societies they depict: recently freed black slaves, in Morrison's case, and India's disenfranchised indigenous minority, in Devi's. By introducing embodied ghosts into otherwise realistically rendered fictional landscapes, these works intentionally disrupt the familiar narrative protocols that allow them to be made meaningful—both those that insist on the mimetic realness of the supernatural events they depict, and those that invite us to read those events metaphorically. But by staging exorcisms, which banish the supernatural and allow characters like Puran, Sethe, and Denver to rejoin the communities from which they had estranged themselves, these works also acknowledge the necessity of compromise: although something is inevitably lost when *Beloved* and "Pterodactyl" are placed into interpretive circulation, something important is gained as well.

Focusing on the novels *Ceremony*, by Leslie Marmon Silko, and *The God of Small Things*, by Arundhati Roy, chapter 2 uses trauma theory to explore how histories of imperial domination refuse to be confined to the past. In both works, the uncanny quality of traumatic memory, which blurs the lines not only between past and present, but also between the ostensibly private sphere of affective experience and the public sphere of the political, raises important questions about the stakes of narrating the past. By inviting identification with its protagonist, *Ceremony* encourages its readers to embrace an alternate narrative of history and share in a healing ceremony that the text itself enacts. *The God of Small Things*, by contrast, expresses a greater suspicion about revisionary narratives, reminding its readers of their responsibility to the past and cautioning them against identifying too easily with its victims. Ultimately, however, my readings of these two works call attention to the oversights of literary trauma theorists who, in their eagerness to give voice to the voiceless, are too readily taken in by the imaginative construct of the third-person narrator. While individual characters may suffer the cognitive distortions of trauma, the fragmentary, nonlinear account that readers receive is, in both novels, mediated by the presence of a narrator whose choices are conscious, volitional, and strategic.

Chapter 3 explores the haunting traces that remain in the wake of political disappearance in the novel *Anil's Ghost*, by Michael Ondaatje, and the American film *Missing* (1982), directed by Costa-Gavras. These works reflect two distinctly different political contexts: *Missing* depicts the 1973 coup that installed Chilean dictator Augusto Pinochet, while *Anil's Ghost* is set in Sri Lanka during the height of that country's civil war, in the late 1980s and early 1990s. Essential to our understanding of these works, I argue, is the recognition of their untimeliness: created and circulated years or decades after the conflicts they depict, their ethical effects are necessarily belated. Both texts rely on the unique properties of fictional narrative to fill the gaps and silences that disappearance produces, creating the disappeared as characters who can be brought to life as mimetically particular individuals or mobilized as abstract types in service of these works' larger thematic ends. While both works ultimately subordinate the mimetic to the thematic, their more troubling erasures are the consequence of their privileged thematic frames. In order to recuperate the American expatriate Charlie Horman as a true victim, rather than a leftist rabble-rouser, *Missing* mobilizes a narrative of American exceptionalism to frame the Chilean coup for a U.S. audience. Written several decades later, *Anil's Ghost* reflects a more cosmopolitan sensibility, appealing to universalistic values of beauty and truth to condemn the violence of Sri Lanka's civil war and elevate the aesthetic as a source of transcendence. While these thematic frameworks allow these works to become meaningful—and ethically consequential—beyond the particular contexts that inspire them, they also exclude entire categories of victims from the compass of their recuperative efforts.

The two works I consider in chapter 4, Ayi Kwei Armah's *The Beautyful Ones Are Not Yet Born* and Don DeLillo's *Falling Man*, look toward a future that is haunted by the unrealized hopes of the past. Neither Armah's depiction of life in newly independent Ghana nor DeLillo's rendering of New York City in the immediate aftermath of 9/11 offer particularly appealing visions of the social worlds these authors occupy. And while a majoritarian writer like DeLillo might seem out of place in this project's archive, his novel's dystopian rendering of the here and now generates an experience of distance and alienation that, as with Armah's text, has been a defining feature of the work's reception: if it is our own world we encounter, in either work, it is not the world we thought we knew. Writing during historical moments in which imagining a different and better future seems both urgently necessary and impossibly compromised, both Armah and DeLillo create texts that transfer that responsibility onto their future readers through their cyclical structure and ambiguous, open-ended narrative. Resisting simplistic forms of optimism, these texts refuse to take up the flawed rhetorics available to them and remain committed to carrying out clear-eyed social critique. But by leaving their representations of societies in crisis open to reinterpretation and rereading, the novels allow for the possibility that the future might offer hopeful visions that are impossible in the present. These texts—and our readings of them—are haunted by the futures that they themselves cannot presage; as readers, we are invited to step into the ghostly reading positions they map out and to question whether we can generate the kinds of genuinely different vision they call for.

Finally, in the conclusion, I suggest the way in which the logic of haunting might recast the stakes, if not the substance, of the world literature debate. Briefly tracing some of the most influential arguments in favor of sameness (in the form of broad circulation and critical expansiveness) and difference (in the form of historical specificity and untranslatability) I suggest that these two opposing positions are both valid and fundamentally irreconcilable. Like the "unmixable mix" of maternal tenderness and reckless rage that gives Roy's Ammu her "Unsafe Edge" (44), works of haunted fiction exemplify both the sameness and the difference through which literature becomes ethically significant. Recognizing that our encounters with works of fiction, like encounters with ghosts, are only temporary allows us to accommodate this kind of instability; ultimately, it is not the text but the reader who is responsible for acting ethically toward others in the nonfictional world. As I hope to show in the chapters that follow, what matters most in the study of world literature is how texts interact with their readers in ways that leave us changed, we hope, for the better.

1

Figures of Estrangement

In Toni Morrison's *Beloved*, a young woman with new clothes and lineless hands walks out of the water and into the kitchen of a former slave; in Mahasweta Devi's novella "Pterodactyl, Puran Sahay, and Pirtha," a prehistoric winged creature takes refuge with a visiting journalist in a remote Indian village. What can these two very differently situated works teach us, together, about the dynamics of literary haunting? Morrison's acclaimed novel about slavery and its aftermath is perhaps the paradigmatic example of haunting in contemporary U.S. ethnic literature. The ghost that takes up residence in Sethe's house on Bluestone Road, on the outskirts of Cincinnati, Ohio, embodies both the consciousness of a murdered child and something more: the collective experience of the Middle Passage and knowledge of the place after death. I intentionally situate Morrison's novel alongside a work that is much less well known to the majority of U.S. readers and critics: Devi's novella, translated from Bengali by Gayatri Spivak, that describes the appearance of a prehistoric creature in an isolated, famine-ravaged tribal community in the Indian state of Bihar. Like Beloved's ghost, the pterodactyl is an otherworldly presence; Puran, the educated, urban journalist who is the work's protagonist, describes it as an ancestral spirit.

Both Beloved and the pterodactyl exemplify the dynamics of haunting as I've described it: an intense, temporary, and ultimately transformative encounter with unfathomable difference. The ghosts in these works are at once incomprehensibly strange and undeniably real, making their presence felt in ways that can't be denied or explained away. Frustrating any attempt at classification or explanation, these ghosts force human characters to confront the limits of their ability to know another. Face-to-face with these incomprehensible creatures, Puran and the residents of 124 Bluestone Road can only care for them, attempting to meet their intense and often insatiable physical and emotional needs. Like these characters, readers of "Pterodactyl" and *Beloved*, in their turn, also confront estranging presences—not ghosts, but depictions of ghosts—that intrude into what otherwise seem to be realistically rendered fictional landscapes. As readers of these works, we encounter ghosts that are insistently, emphatically real; both Beloved and the pterodactyl, despite their obvious symbolic resonances, are depicted first and foremost as concrete, particular, physical presences. This mimetic investment in the supernatural, largely devoid of the generic or interpretive infrastructure that typically accompanies it, creates an unsettling experience for these works' readers that is not unlike what the characters themselves endure. Like Sethe, Denver, and Puran, we find ourselves confronted by presences and phenomena that, in their shocking and insistent immediacy, resist established forms of literary meaning-making.

The ghosts in these works are ambivalent figures: while they inspire characters like Puran and Sethe to discover new ways of relating to others, the effort to connect with these impossible creatures across profound difference proves endlessly circular and, ultimately, unsustainable. Puran, despite his repeated efforts, cannot plumb the depths of the pterodactyl's gaze; he can only conceal its body in a cavern where it will be protected from the prying eyes of the outside world. Sethe and Denver similarly cannot coexist with a ghost; on the brink of starvation, terrorized by Beloved's violent tantrums, they must drive the mysterious young woman out of the house on Bluestone Road in order to survive. In both works, these acts of literal or figurative exorcism make way for more effective—if admittedly imperfect and incomplete—forms of communication that can be productively received and acted upon by others: Puran writes a conventional journalistic exposé of the official mismanagement in Pirtha, and Denver and Paul D. learn to tell stories that allow others to form their own opinions. Similarly, these works themselves enter into circulation—productively—in a variety of ways, through readings that inevitably contain or efface some element of their underlying instability. Although admittedly selective, I argue, these interpretations are not instances of misreading; far from it, they enact precisely the kind of strategic engagements with alterity that the texts themselves both authorize and demand.

The Limits of Knowledge in the Haunting Encounter

Both Devi's novella and Morrison's novel are deeply invested in the relationship between knowledge and storytelling. In both these works, storytelling is presented as a potentially pernicious exercise of power. For Puran, information gleaned from reference books becomes a stand-in for more genuine forms of connection; his encounters with the pterodactyl and the people of Pirtha, however, quickly reveal his sense of confidence and self-sufficiency to be misplaced. In a similar way, the members of the family at 124 Bluestone Road fall victim to their own mistaken certainties about others and the world around them, acting on assumptions in ways that harm them and erode the sustaining bonds of their community. As writers who themselves tell the stories of marginalized characters to readers at a distance, Morrison and Devi are understandably concerned about the asymmetries of power that such acts of storytelling might entail. Morrison's novel brings to life a chapter in America's past that many would prefer to forget; Devi takes as her subject the indigenous communities not merely left out of, but actively harmed by, the economic and political structures of the modern Indian nation. Not surprisingly, therefore, the encounters across difference that they depict offer powerful lessons about how such boundary-crossing texts should be read and about the conditions of possibility of their imaginative interventions: as works of fiction, they require us to abandon the desire for knowledge and to accept something fundamentally different in its place.

At the start of Devi's novella, Puran is portrayed as a man adrift in his own life. An educated, middle-class journalist who works for a local newspaper in the city of Patna, Puran has paid little attention to his personal and family life. A widower, he has allowed his son, whose mother died in childbirth, to be raised primarily by his grandmother. And although Puran has been with his girlfriend, Saraswati, for fourteen years, they have not married, and he is the first to admit that "no real relationship has grown" between them.[1] Shortly before Puran's departure to cover the famine in Pirtha, Saraswati has issued him an ultimatum: still unmarried at the age of thirty-two, she is ready to give up on him and join an ashram. Puran acknowledges that he is responsible for not allowing "a fleshly, hungry, thirsty, human relationship to grow" between him and Saraswati, but feels unable to do anything about it and ponders the following "moral question": "how will a person merely floating in the every-day world, who has not attempted to build a human relationship with mother-son-Saraswati, be able to do justice to a subject as a journalist?" (97).

Indeed, although Puran prides himself on his efforts to advocate for members of India's tribal minority and other oppressed groups through his journalism, he fears he has become "altogether too professional" of late, transitioning easily from hard-nosed investigative reporting to writing glib promotional pieces such as "Bihar, A Tourist's Paradise" (98). And although Puran's political writings have received praise, the text makes clear how little Puran understands about the experiences and values of the tribal people he attempts to represent: writing about a tribal man who attacked another man in a conflict over a water buffalo, Puran cannot understand why such a seemingly minor disagreement would become violent—despite the attacker's explanation that a water buffalo is invaluable to a farmer—and congratulates himself for turning the man's life-and-death story into "a most compassionate small news item" (103). Reflecting on the episode later, Puran realizes that he "had not grasped the desperation behind [the man's] urgent and troubled message" (103). Rather than listening to the man and relating to him in a meaningful way, Puran adopts a distant viewpoint that makes him an object of pity for an audience of comparatively privileged newspaper readers.

Devi's novella suggests that Puran's shortcomings, both as a romantic partner and as an activist journalist, derive from the way he attempts to relate to others—as objects of knowledge that can be mastered. There's more than a little truth in Saraswati's teasing when she suggests to him that "perhaps you have not been able to know me after so many years spent close together because there is no book about me" (158). Indeed, Puran credits himself with having "done his homework" to prepare for his trip to Pirtha by reading reference materials about the geography and economy of the Madhya Pradesh region and "the characteristics of the Indian Austric"—India's ethnically and culturally distinct, and historically disenfranchised, minority population (108, 114). He fails to imagine, however, that these demographic differences might give rise to an experience of the world that is profoundly different from his own. The tribal people living in Pirtha and other neighboring towns are dying from a man-made famine and from pesticide poisoning; Puran's friend Harisharan, a local official, has invited him there hoping to publicize the humanitarian crisis and obtain relief supplies for his starving constituents. Armed only with abstract knowledge of this poverty, Puran misguidedly endeavors to emulate it, taking pride in the minimalism of his travel bag and insisting on only rudimentary food and lodging, rather than the comparatively comfortable accommodations that he, as a guest in the community, is first offered. Such self-denial, however, misses the point: when Puran tries to avoid eating dinner, Shankar, an educated tribal man, bluntly informs him that "you people understand nothing. Will our hunger lessen if you don't eat?" (136). Shankar's bitter observation reveals what Puran fails to acknowledge: that all hunger is not equivalent, and his voluntary self-deprivation has a fundamentally different significance than the tribals' starvation.

Eventually, however, Puran starts to realize how little he understands about the lives of those whose suffering he has come to document. After his conversation with Shankar, he recognizes the futility of superficial gestures like refusing food or theatrically handing over his camera, which do nothing to bring him closer to the people of Pirtha: "He had always thought he was altogether self-reliant since he set out with nothing but a sarong and a toothbrush in his shoulder bag. Now he sees that's not enough. He feels inadequate. It's true that he can't reach Shankar's people by eating little or sleeping on grass mats. There is a great gulf fixed between Puran's kind and Shankar's kind. But he does want to get close" (140). In this moment, Puran becomes aware that his abstract knowledge of tribal life has not prepared him to connect with the people of Pirtha in any meaningful way. Something different, he realizes, is necessary to bridge the gap between them—a fact that Saraswati has long understood: "Some day you'll see that what you know is not enough," she predicts. "Then perhaps your pride will fall, and you'll act natural" (140).

This dawning awareness is crystallized by Puran's encounter with the birdlike prehistoric creature that appears in the hut where he is sleeping on his first night in Pirtha. His initial reaction is utter incomprehension; it's as if he had seen "a stone flying" (141). The existence of the pterodactyl violates Puran's most basic assumptions about the world he inhabits, and consulting a reference book on dinosaurs doesn't help: the book describes no creature quite like the one he has seen, nor does it explain how a living dinosaur could exist in modern India. Faced with the inadequacy of his knowledge, Puran abandons his efforts to learn about the pterodactyl and tries instead to communicate with it, gazing into its eyes and attempting to interpret what he sees there. Despite his concerted efforts, however, the pterodactyl remains fundamentally inscrutable: there is "no communication between [their] eyes. Only a dusky waiting, without end" (157).

Although the pterodactyl remains utterly mysterious to Puran, his connection with the creature is direct, immediate, and even intimate: he conceals it in the hut where he himself is sleeping and endeavors to feed it from his own allotment of food. (At one point, Puran asks Harisharan for fish to eat, and although Harisharan quickly brushes off his friend's outlandish request, the attentive reader recognizes that the fish is intended to feed the pterodactyl.) Together, Puran and Bikhia, the tribal boy who first sighted the creature, attempt to care for the pterodactyl, searching unsuccessfully for food that it might eat and protecting it from the prying eyes of the outside world. Though less definitive than the "knowledge" contained in his inadequate reference book, Puran's efforts to meet the pterodactyl's needs are a far more meaningful form of connection across difference. Addressing the creature, he muses, "You've come to me for shelter, and I don't know how to save you, is that why I'll see your death?" (158). "I don't know," he repeats, again and again, and in abandoning his efforts to know the pterodactyl, he feels a connection and an obligation to the creature that derives from its alterity rather than his own attempt at mastery (158).

Much as the appearance of the pterodactyl forces Puran to abandon superficial forms of knowledge in favor of an engagement with the creature in all its difference, *Beloved*'s ghost leads Morrison's characters to question their own certainties about others. As many critics have noted, Morrison's novel expresses a deep-seated concern with knowledge as an exercise of power.[2] *Beloved* is replete with characters who claim to know—and thus feel empowered to judge—those around them. Sethe is made the object of knowledge, first by schoolteacher, the slave master who asks his pupils to list her "animal" and "human characteristics,"[3] and later by the black community, including Paul D., who accuses her of inhumanity when he learns of her act of infanticide. But Sethe is also brought low by her own assumptions that she can know others: her children, her neighbors, and the ghost that takes up residence in her home.

Much has been made of Sethe's coinage "rememory" (38), which attests to the repetitive, open-ended quality of memory in Morrison's novel and, more generally, the haunting quality of the traumatic past, which I explore at length in chapter 2.[4] Less re-marked upon is the fact that Sethe's particular understanding of the past as contagious also allows her to claim definitive knowledge of her children's futures and thus assert control over their lives and choices in the present. As Sethe explains to Denver, memories are not confined to the minds of those who formed them. "If a house burns down, it's gone, but the place—the picture of it—stays, and not just in my rememory, but out there, in the world," where other people can encounter it (38). For that reason, she explains, Denver can never go back to Sweet Home, the plantation from which Sethe and her older children escaped: "if you go there—you who never was there—if you go there and stand in the place where it was, it will happen again; it will be there for you, waiting for you" (38). Sethe's concern that her own past will inevitably be repeated by her daughter fails to recognize Denver's status as an individual, denying her the autonomy to experience events differently and the agency to make different choices than her mother did. It is this presumed certainty about her children's fates that ultimately mo-tivates Sethe to take their lives into her own hands.

Sethe's act of infanticide, which takes place prior to the nov-el's main events, is the emotional, ethical, and narrative core of *Beloved*. Having escaped to freedom, Sethe acts decisively when threatened with recapture: she "splits to the woodshed to kill her children" and is able to take the life of one of her two daughters before anyone can stop her (166). Although the violence of Sethe's act is extreme, it is not the violence itself that most troubles Sethe's family and community. The free black community in Cincinnati harbors no illusions about the harshness of the world they inhabit, in which the primary source of gainful employment is the slaugh-terhouse, and small horrors like the discovery of "a red ribbon knotted around a curl of wet wooly hair, still clinging to its bit of scalp," are a quotidian occurrence (189). Violence may be unavoidable, even necessary, in such a world; those close to Sethe, however, recognize and reject not simply the violence of her actions but, instead, the totalizing nature of her claim over her children.

Perversely echoing the possessive logic of slavery, Sethe views her children not as sovereign individuals, but rather as part of herself: "The best thing she was, was her children. Whites might dirty *her*, all right, but not her best thing, her beautiful, magical best thing—the part of her that was clean" (264). Paul D.'s reaction to this logic typifies that of the community at large: "more important than what Sethe had done was what she claimed. It scared him" (172). Ultimately, Morrison makes clear, it is not the haunting of 124 itself that has isolated the family from their neighbors and from one another, but rather the kind of claim to know another that Sethe's act of infanticide asserts. In her certainty that she knows best for her children, Sethe fails to imagine how they might experience her violent actions; as a result, they live in constant fear of her. "All the time, I'm afraid the thing that happened that made it all right for my mother to kill my sister could happen again," Denver explains (215); and it is not frustration with their haunted house, as the novel initially implies, but rather fear of their mother that drives the two older boys, Howard and Buglar, to leave home.

Sethe is not the only person at 124, or in Morrison's black Cincinnati, who makes assumptions or rushes to judgment. When Nelson Lord, a classmate, asks Denver an innocent question about her mother's imprisonment, Denver goes temporarily deaf to avoid hearing comments she assumes will be hurtful. And Paul D., certain he knows Sethe better than anyone, ardently denies that she could be the woman pictured in the newspaper clipping that their neighbor, Stamp Paid, shows him; when he discovers that she is not the "obedient," "shy," and "work-crazy" girl he thought he knew from their time at Sweet Home (173), he accuses her of being no better than an animal and leaves her. Morrison makes it clear that these sorts of assumptions not only isolate characters from one another but also, in doing so, disrupt the network of sustaining relationships that the embattled black community relies on for its survival. Indeed, Sethe's crime itself might have been avoided had the family been alerted to the slave catchers' approach, but the standoffishness of Sethe's neighbors, who impute pridefulness to the family and their actions, prevents such a warning from being sent.

Much as the pterodactyl's impossible appearance forces Puran to reevaluate his own certainties, the young woman who appears outside the house at 124 Bluestone Road defies all attempts at explanation and demonstrates the inadequacy of any assumptions made about her. When she first arrives, helpless, confused, and insatiably thirsty, Paul D. and Sethe theorize that Beloved has fled someone or something terrible, but her clean, fine clothes and baby-soft feet seem to rule out an arduous escape on foot. Although they initially attribute her fever, cough, and thirst to cholera, her symptoms defy diagnosis, and her continued frailty and dependence contrast with surprising feats of nearly superhuman strength; Paul D. muses, bewildered, that Beloved "can't walk, but I seen her pick up the rocker with one hand" (59). Her childlike behavior—babbling, playing games, and throwing tantrums—is at odds with her calculated efforts to seduce Paul D. and drive him away from Sethe. Most importantly, although both Sethe and Denver become convinced that Beloved is the ghost of Sethe's murdered daughter, the two women's certainty is never fully endorsed by the novel. Although Beloved remembers things, like Sethe's special song, that only her child could know, she also knows things that exceed Sethe's grasp, such as the nature of the "dark place" she was in before, which merges a vision of death with the experiences of slaves on the Middle Passage (264). In retrospect, Denver believes at times that Beloved was "sure 'nough [her] sister," but reflects that "at times I think she was—more" (281).

In both "Pterodactyl" and *Beloved*, the appearance of supernatural creatures reveals the limits of the knowledge-making systems on which characters like Puran and Sethe have relied to make sense of the world they inhabit; in a similar way, I want to suggest, the ghosts in these works destabilize meaning-making schema for their readers as well. It's not simply that "Pterodactyl" and *Beloved* depart from the conventions of literary realism or historical fiction by including ghosts; rather, it's the particular way they present them: these works are invested in depicting the supernatural entities they imagine as mimetically real, particularized figures, but at the same time, they withhold the naturalizing structures of genre that might facilitate readers' engagements with such estranging elements. To the extent that these fictional ghosts defy existing interpretive paradigms, I contend, they resist being put into symbolic circulation; the result is our own unsettling encounter—resembling Puran's and Sethe's—with texts that resist abstraction and generalization and require, instead, more demanding forms of contact and accommodation.

Interpreting the Supernatural

Fiction is not real; that's true whether or not the work in question contains ghosts or other supernatural phenomena. In a realist work, the characters we encounter are not actually existing people, but fictional representations of people who could exist, whose stories are engaging to the extent that they are persuasively individual, but useful to the extent that they can be productively generalized. Given this fact, the reading practices of literary critics overwhelmingly privilege the thematic dimension of fiction, deploying interpretive schema that allow the particularities of fictional worlds to be put into circulation as ideas.[5] Mimetic reading holds the potential to deflate these sorts of thematic arguments, reducing symbolically or ideologically significant authorial choices to mere reflections of the external world. (Consider the innumerable classroom discussions that have run aground on assertions like "it's believable that he would act that way," or "maybe that's just what it was like back then," which privilege the mimetic at the expense of the thematic.) In the particular case of fiction from the margins, however, mimetic "realness" assumes a special importance to readers and literary critics alike: if a certain group of people or category of experiences has been systematically written out of history, there is indeed value in writing them back in, and when navigating a representational space marked by pernicious stereotypes, accuracy matters.

Part of what we might hope a work like *Beloved* or "Pterodactyl" will do, therefore, even before we make it meaningful on a thematic or symbolic level, is help us imagine what it would be like to be a person so positioned—a recently emancipated slave or an illiterate Indian tribal. Indeed, Devi explains, in an interview included in the English edition of *Imaginary Maps*, that she intends her fiction to serve as a corrective, restoring the stories of tribals that are omitted from familiar narratives of Indian national history. She recalls, "A tribal girl asked me modestly: 'When we go to school, we read about Mahatma Gandhi. Did we have no heroes? Did we always suffer like this?' That is why I started writing about the tribal movements and the tribal heroes."[6] Devi's account of writing to fill a gap in the historical record echoes Morrison's oft-cited explanation of her own goals as a writer of fiction. In the written accounts of slavery that exist, she points out, there's little record of the subjective experience of slaves themselves, who often wrote strategically or under conditions of censorship. According to Morrison, then, the task of the fiction writer is "to find and expose a truth about the interior life of people who didn't write it."[7] As their own statements suggest, therefore, both writers are explicitly committed to mimetic representation as a strategy for recovering the silenced stories of those at society's margins.

Magical elements like baby ghosts or modern-day dinosaurs trouble this project, for several reasons. We might worry, for one, that such elements could distort readers' perceptions of the lives and experiences of others at a distance, or perhaps even be taken to suggest that the reality they inhabit differs in fundamental ways from readers' own. This is the kind of fallacy that, Frederick Aldama observes, permeates the scholarship on magical realism; critics of these works, he suggests, frequently conflate narrative strategies (Third World writers create fictional storyworlds imbued with magic) with ontological claims (the actually existing Third World is innately magical).[8] This kind of reading illustrates the logic of difference carried to its extreme: a willingness, or even an exotifying desire, to imagine that the world inhabited by social and cultural others is so totally unknowable that it might well operate according to different metaphysical rules. Another understandable concern is that introducing magical elements into otherwise realistic fictional worlds might obscure our understanding of historical causality. Focusing on ghosts is indeed a mistake if it leads us to respond to slavery's legacies by holding séances rather than instituting affirmative action programs—in other words, if it conceals the mechanisms through which power has operated in the past and continues to operate in the present.

Aldama is correct to insist on the distinction between onto-logical facts and aesthetic strategies: to interpret magical elements in imagined worlds as strictly, empirically true misconstrues the nature of fictional storytelling. That doesn't mean, however, that works like "Pterodactyl" and *Beloved* aren't invested in represent-ing their ghosts mimetically, with all the detail and particularity of a real referent or a believable character. While it might seem para-doxical to talk about mimetically representing things that don't exist, that's precisely what genres like science fiction, fantasy, magi-cal realism, and horror do: they take the particularities of their impossible characters and events seriously, and the concrete reality of these supernatural elements within the storyworld is necessary to their narrative functioning. Indeed, following Seo-Young Chu's persuasive argument, the imaginative work involved in represent-ing real and unreal objects is different not in kind, but rather in degree. To the extent that all referents—whether pencils or space ships—resist being perfectly captured in fictional language, the imaginative leap required to accept the appearance of dinosaurs or baby ghosts is not qualitatively different from that required to visualize the contents of Puran's travel bag or imagine the itching sensation of chamomile sap on Sethe's legs.[9] Thus, the intrusion of ghosts in "Pterodactyl" and *Beloved* does not necessarily signal a departure from the conventions of mimetic representation; rather, it requires readers to move from what Chu would describe as the "low intensity" imaginative work required to mimetically render the worlds of Pirtha or Cincinnati to the comparatively "high in-tensity" task of conjuring a prehistoric winged creature or an ap-paritional young woman with lineless hands.[10]

Notably, therefore, the supernatural creatures in both *Beloved* and "Pterodactyl" are presented first and foremost as mate-rial beings, characters with specific, individuating attributes and practical physical needs. Devi's depiction of the pterodactyl is rich in physical detail: it is larger than a sparrow, but its wingspan is less than twenty-five feet; it is toothless and tailless (unlike the prehistoric creatures described in Puran's reference book), its eyes are gray, and it has a noticeable, "carnal" smell (154). It has arrived wounded, with a damaged wing that it drags as it walks, a particular, limping motion that Bikhia carefully mimes for Puran. And it is slowly starving to death, despite the variety of foods that the two contrive to bring to it: rice, kodo, grass, small fish, and even a snake Bikhia manages to catch. The young woman who appears at 124 is also hungry, with a particular taste for sweets. Beloved loves "honey as well as the wax it came in, sugar sandwiches, the sludgy molasses gone hard and brutal in the can, lemonade, taffy, and any type of dessert" (58), and the novel's account of her food preferences parallels Baby Suggs's recollection of her own long-lost child, individualized in her fading memory by a taste for "the burned bottom of bread" (146). Beloved's lineless skin, asthmatic breathing, saucer-thin neck, and eventually her pregnant belly, "protruding like a winning watermelon," are described in vivid detail, and the violent consequences of her tantrums, throwing chairs and clawing at her throat until "rubies of blood" appear, are made equally tangible and concrete (263). To say that the pterodactyl embodies a threatened tribal way of life, or that Beloved represents the traumas of slavery, fails to account for the concrete, physical attributes that bring these characters to life as specific, embodied creatures, rather than mere abstractions.

Despite this wealth of detail, the material realness (and strangeness) of these supernatural figures is downplayed in scholarly readings that emphasize their symbolic significance, allowing Morrison's novel and Devi's novella to fit more comfortably into the category of serious literary fiction. As Jan Alber has suggested, the distinction between mimetic and thematic investments in the supernatural is often manifested through genre: works in which supernatural figures or phenomena are mimetically important are likely to be read as examples of horror, science fiction, fantasy, or the gothic—low- rather than high-cultural forms.[11] These genre distinctions become visible in interesting ways, as Ruby Tapia points out, when *Beloved* moves from the page to the screen, and the embodied strangeness of the ghost rendered in Morrison's prose becomes undeniably concrete in Thandie Newton's performance as the title character.[12] For many of its viewers, the film's emphasis on the mimetic registers as a shift in genre, from historical fiction to horror; academic readers familiar with Morrison's novel, in particular, often come away from the film discomfited by the literalness of attributes like Beloved's strange, scratchy voice that are clearly specified, but typically overlooked, in the written text. Although certain readers of the novel may conveniently forget them, these are precisely the details that prevent the supernatural elements in *Beloved*, like those in "Pterodactyl," from being contained and neutralized as purely symbolic.

If these ghosts resist being read solely, or even primarily, as metaphors, what prevents us from making sense of them, as we might other supernatural elements, through the narrative conventions of genre fiction? As Alber observes, readers who encounter "unnatural" elements in works of fiction have a range of options: one is to interpret those elements as symbolic or allegorical; another is to naturalize those elements through the conventions of specific genres, like magical realism, science fiction, fantasy, or horror, in which the mimetic "realness" of unnatural characters and events is a foundational conceit.[13] Such a commitment to mimetically representing so-called estranging or impossible referents is, for example, one of the hallmarks of science fiction; as noted science fiction writer Samuel Delany has remarked, the conventions of the genre prompt its readers to take literally the kinds of figurative language—for instance, "her world exploded"—that might otherwise be construed as metaphor.[14] Alternatively, magical realism might seem to be an apt way to classify the storyworlds in both *Beloved* and "Pterodactyl," in which a few magical elements punctuate an otherwise realistically rendered fictional landscape. Despite containing elements suggestive of various genres, however, neither *Beloved* nor "Pterodactyl" can, I contend, be comfortably assimilated into any of these preexisting meaning-making structures, for reasons I will outline below.

Although *Beloved*, in particular, is frequently read through the lens of magical realism, both Morrison's and Devi's texts diverge from the conventions of this genre in significant ways.[15] Unlike magical realist works, in which, following Wendy Faris's familiar definition, "the marvelous seems to grow organically within the ordinary," *Beloved* and "Pterodactyl" both describe and inspire doubt about the supernatural phenomena they depict.[16] Puran experiences a mental "explosion" when he first sees the pterodactyl (159), and Paul D. is genuinely mystified by Beloved's inexplicable combination of helplessness and strength. As these examples illustrate, neither *Beloved* nor "Pterodactyl" present magic as an ordinary and accepted part of the fictional storyworld; rather, for characters like Puran and Paul D., and by extension, these works' readers, it requires an explanation—one that the works themselves consistently fail to provide. This lack of explanation also distinguishes these works, in turn, from the genres of fantasy and science fiction, which are invested, often deeply, in providing detailed, logical, and internally consistent explanations of the supernatural elements they depict.[17] Notably, "Pterodactyl" offers no *Jurassic Park*–like description of dinosaur DNA encased in amber, and *Beloved* provides no careful explication of the mechanism by which souls with unfinished business are prevented from crossing over; rather than justifying supernatural elements as rationally explicable features of their fictional storyworlds, these works allow them to remain fundamentally mysterious. Thus, although "Pterodactyl" and *Beloved* ask their readers to understand their ghosts as diegetically real, we're given none of the familiar kinds of generic infrastructure that typically facilitate doing so.

Genre conventions are a mechanism by which literary texts codify and invite certain practices of interpretation; for the science fiction reader who knows that "her world exploded" is not a metaphor, the act of suspending disbelief to imagine an exploded world also situates that world, explicitly or implicitly, in relation to the reader's own. Such orientation is impossible in *Beloved* and "Pterodactyl"; in their resistance to interpretation through genre or any other thematic paradigm, they display what H. Porter Abbott has aptly characterized as the "palpable unknown," "a form of recalcitrance designed to immerse the reader in a state of unknowing, robbed not only of cognitive mastery but of its resources."[18] As Abbott suggests, these works intentionally resist the work of interpretation, "lead[ing] us not simply to acknowledge that we don't know but to feel the insistent presence of this condition. It is a humbling experience."[19] Like Puran and the characters in Morrison's novel, we are forced by this encounter with the unknowable to recognize the limits of abstract, rational meaning-making, to discover new ways of relating, and to enter into a form of direct, personal contact that does not assert claims of mastery. When we cannot know the text, we can only feel with it.

By obstructing the reader's impulse to interpret in this way, therefore, these fictional works carry out ethical maneuvers analogous to the ones they depict, restricting forms of knowledge making that seek to dominate their objects, and calling instead for intimate contact with unsettling and unknowable complexity. But, parting ways with Abbott, I contend that such a reading practice, which embraces uncertainty, also has important and necessary limits. In the absence of countervailing forces, the recalcitrance he attributes to works like *Beloved* and "Pterodactyl" can result in a kind of paralysis: if all interpretations do violence to the text, how are we to build meaningful bridges from the fictional world to the real one? Although feeling with the text may be a powerful and even transformative experience, it is, by definition, not a portable one. There's value, therefore, in interpreting even those texts that consistently frustrate the readerly impulse toward generalization and abstraction. And indeed, despite their resistance, both *Beloved* and "Pterodactyl" have been read, interpreted, and made meaningful, over and over again, in a wide range of contexts.

In fact, I would argue that these works implicitly authorize the kinds of compromises that are necessary to put them into interpretive circulation. As Puran and the residents of 124 Bluestone Road quickly realize, haunting comes at a cost: while the face-to-face encounter with the ghost may offer an alternative to dominating forms of knowledge making, it can also be dangerously circular—neither the pterodactyl nor Beloved can be made understandable, nor made to understand. By scrambling the forms of communication that allow individuals to move forward and communities to draw together, these ghosts ultimately threaten the survival of the living. As a result, both works conclude with exorcisms that bring their haunting encounters to a close and authorize a return to the ordinary social world: to more fruitful forms of communication and more reciprocal relationships with others. The stories these surviving characters tell, once freed from the cycles of fruitless narration their encounters with ghosts inspired, are partial and inadequate but also profoundly necessary. Changed and, importantly, humbled by their experiences, Puran and the residents of 124 more readily recognize the compromises inherent in their communications and interactions with others. By telling stories of haunting and of exorcism, these two fictional works authorize precisely the kinds of readings to which they are inevitably subjected—readings that, though selective or strategic, allow them to be made useful in the wider world.

The Necessity of Exorcism

If the strangeness of ghosts shatters characters' illusions of certainty and brings them into dialogue, it also renders the ghosts' continued presence unsustainable: as otherworldly presences, they lie too far beyond these characters' experiences to be comprehended. In both works, therefore, the effort to discern and satisfy the ghosts' needs is a never-ending process that threatens to consume the living: Sethe, Denver, and Beloved become "locked in a love that wore everybody out" (255), and Puran quickly recognizes "the intolerable burden of his explosive discovery" (143). In each case, therefore, an exorcism is necessary to free these characters from their all-consuming encounters and allow them to reenter the social worlds they've left behind, forever changed by their experiences. No longer overconfident in their knowledge of others, Puran and the family at 124 are newly willing to engage in dialogue, but they also recognize that dialogue has its limits. Chastened by their costly and futile attempts to comprehend the incomprehensible, they now recognize that in any dialogue there is something that cannot be communicated—what Devi's text describes as an "asymptote" (102)—and embrace the imperfect, strategic narratives that provide the basis for productive personal and social engagement.

The exorcism at the conclusion of Morrison's novel is at least as well known as the haunting at its center: although at first the women at 124 welcome the return of their lost daughter and sister, it quickly becomes clear that Beloved's presence is more taxing than sustaining. Looking into Beloved's eyes, "the longing that [Sethe] saw there was bottomless" (62). Beloved's insatiable appetites for food, love, and attention quickly exhaust Sethe's and Denver's meager resources. Eager to please the ghost of her "lonely and rebuked" child, Sethe quits her job, spends her savings recklessly on gaudy fabrics and trims, and plants flowers in her vegetable garden for Beloved to enjoy (14). As Denver comes to understand, however, Beloved's desires cannot be reduced to—or satisfied by—the women's material and emotional offerings: "Deep down in her wide black eyes, back behind the expressionlessness, was a palm held out for a penny that Denver would gladly give her, if only she knew how or knew enough about her" (124). And there is no saying no to Beloved, who flies into a rage whenever Sethe tries to exercise parental authority: "Anything she wanted she got, and when Sethe ran out of things to give her, Beloved invented desire" (253). No attempt to satisfy Beloved can be sufficient, and their ceaseless, futile efforts leave the women on the brink of exhaustion and starvation.

In a similar way, Beloved displays an insatiable demand for stories and explanations but is never satisfied by them. When she first recognizes Beloved as the embodiment of her lost daughter, Sethe believes she will finally be able to explain what she never saw the need to before: why her act of murder was at heart an act of love. And although she initially takes comfort from the thought that she can finally forget the most painful parts of her past, the opposite proves to be true; with Beloved as her interlocutor, Sethe's stories devolve into endless, repetitive cycles. Like her (literally and figuratively) circling attempt to explain her act of infanticide to Paul D., Sethe's stories go on and on, yet yield no understanding. Her greatest fear is that Beloved will leave "before Sethe could make her understand what it meant—what it took to drag the teeth of the saw under the little chin; to feel the baby blood pump like oil in her hands" (264). Despite Sethe's incessant attempts to explain, however, Beloved remains "uncomprehending," and the stories she offers in return, about "the other side," a dark, hot place where she and others are surrounded by "men without skin," utterly exceed Sethe's grasp (226, 264). Instead of bringing them closer together, this exchange of stories only fuels the escalating violence of Beloved's tantrums. Together, Beloved and Sethe perform endless rounds of fruitless narration: disjointed, circular conversations, rendered in striking chapters near the conclusion of the novel.

Ultimately, it's Denver's willingness to tell a partial story that allows the family to survive. In her courageous ventures out into the world beyond her yard, Denver learns to offer information and gratitude, and receives food and acceptance from neighbors in exchange. Unlike Sethe, who refuses to explain herself to the black community, on the one hand, and offers explanation without end to Beloved, on the other, Denver realizes that she needs to tell a story that others can understand and relate to. "Nobody was going to help her unless she told it—all of it," she acknowledges; but even so, Denver does not provide a full account, and "explained the girl in her house who plagued her mother as a cousin come to visit, who got sick too and bothered them both" (266, 267). By recognizing the limits of her ability to narrate her experiences, and telling others only what they need to know, Denver moves beyond the endless cycle in which Sethe and Beloved are locked and elicits the compassion and support her family so desperately needs.

In fact, it is precisely the open-endedness of Denver's story that enables the other women to rally to Sethe's defense. From the scant information that Denver provides, and her reluctant admission that the troublesome "cousin" has lineless hands, the women construct an outrageous account of 124's haunting that, while falling fairly close to the mark, is entirely fabricated. Each woman, in turn, interprets the story to her own purposes. Ella, for instance, compares Sethe's murdered daughter to her own infant, conceived through rape, whom she refused to nurse. There is, therefore, "something very personal in her fury" at the past's intolerable invasion of the present in the form of Beloved's ghost; although she sees Sethe herself as "too complicated" and her actions as "prideful [and] misdirected," Ella nevertheless shares an interest in keeping the ghosts of the past at bay (269). Morrison suggests that each of the women who join in the exorcism party, similarly, does so for her own reasons. Gathered together outside 124, the women's distinct voices come together in a perfect and powerful harmony that drives Beloved's ghost—naked and swollen in pregnancy—running from the house, never to be seen or heard from again.

If Beloved's haunting presence traps the residents of 124 in endless and ultimately fruitless attempts to communicate the true nature of their experience, her exorcism frees them to form relationships with others that acknowledge difference without seeking to erase it completely. In the final pages of the novel, Denver has fully entered the world she and her mother so feared—working, building relationships, and preparing to possibly attend college. Nelson Lord, whose question about her past once caused Denver to go temporarily deaf, now kindles her romantic interest, and the prospect of such a relationship shows how much the formerly reclusive Denver has changed. When she tells Paul D. of her college plans, he resists warning her that "nothing in the world more dangerous than a white schoolteacher" (280), as he might have done before. Instead, he acknowledges that Denver's experience might differ from his own, and when she raises the question of his relationship with Beloved—a touchy subject for them both—he recognizes her right to form her own opinion. And although Sethe has been brought low by Beloved's haunting, her tentative response to Paul D.'s insistence that "you your best thing" holds the possibility that she, too, may come to recognize and value the difference that separates her from her children (288).

Although it does not require the kind of dramatic exorcism that banishes Beloved's ghost, Devi's pterodactyl also cannot reside permanently in the world of the living, and confronting its impossible strangeness can have unsettling or even dangerous consequences, as the story of another journalist, Surajpratap, illustrates. Surajpratap, an idealist and reformer who made a reputation for himself in the Dalit (or "Untouchable") movement, arrives in Pirtha before Puran, shortly after Bikhia's initial sighting of the pterodactyl. When he photographs Bikhia's carved likeness of the pterodactyl and attempts to publish a story about it, Harisharan and the Sub-Division Officer confiscate his film, and he loses his job at the government-connected newspaper where he works. Ultimately, Surajpratap suffers a nervous breakdown; a man who "had great promise," he drops out of sight and achieves nothing for the people of Pirtha (112). The "explosion in . . . Surajpratap's head" (159) when he sees the carving exemplifies the danger of trying to know the inscrutable pterodactyl, and the political reprisal he faces demonstrates the personal cost and ultimate futility of attempting to tell an unedited version of its story.

For Puran, as for Surajpratap, the discovery of the pterodactyl is "explosive" (143)—potentially destructive in its incomprehensibility—and Puran struggles to make the creature's appearance meaningful by discerning in its gaze some kind of concrete political or ethical message. He poses many possible explanations to the creature and to himself, including that man-made famine is a crime, that the "collective being" of tribal peoples has been crushed, and that humans, like dinosaurs, are becoming an endangered species in the modern era (157). Significantly, however, neither the pterodactyl nor the text itself sanctions any of these interpretations, and to each of Puran's questions the creature's "dusky lidless eyes remain unresponsive" (157). Eventually, Puran, unlike Surajpratap, realizes that the pterodactyl is, in its absolute strangeness, beyond his reach: "I won't go near, I won't touch you, I will not take your picture with the flash bulb of my camera," he reassures the creature (155). Unable to prevent the pterodactyl's death, he and Bikhia conspire to conceal its body, and so shield Pirtha from the unwanted attention of the outside world, which would no doubt sensationalize its discovery and wreak havoc on the already precarious life of the tribal community.

Much like Denver's haunting encounter, Puran's time in Pirtha teaches him to recognize that communication is imperfect and knowledge is always incomplete. Changed by his encounter with the pterodactyl, Puran comes to understand that he can only fulfill his responsibility to the tribal community by embracing the compromises inherent in his work as a journalist: "Pirtha has taught him that, even if you are a reporter, you must not ask all the questions all the time" (180). The story that he writes, therefore, is a scathing indictment of the exploitation, corruption, and disenfranchisement that cause people in places like Pirtha to starve while other parts of the nation prosper, and makes no mention of the pterodactyl. On its face, Puran's article about Pirtha may not differ greatly from his earlier "compassionate small-news item" (103). This time, however, he recognizes and even exploits its inevitable silences and omissions, consciously juxtaposing images of tribal abjection with captions that echo the glib language of international development and government sloganeering; as he explains to Harisharan, "these pictures will reveal some truths and some lies" (192). Unlike Surajpratap, Puran recognizes the value of a compromised narrative that might bring material aid to the people of Pirtha, and after his transformative encounter with the pterodactyl, he embraces his role as an outsider who can create and circulate such necessary fictions.

Puran's confrontation with the pterodactyl's unfathomable strangeness has lasting effects on his personal relationships, as well. The bond Puran forges with Bikhia, in particular, contrasts sharply with his earlier efforts to connect with the tribals. As the pterodactyl's caretakers, Puran and Bikhia are bound together by necessity in a tacit partnership; by the time Puran leaves Pirtha, however, he has come to recognize and value the irreducible distance between them. Meeting eyes with Bikhia, Puran infers the cautionary message that despite their provisional alliance, "you remain you, and I remain me, and after this heavy phase is over each will return to the orbit of his life" (182). His compliance with Bikhia's directives—that he participate in traditional mourning rituals to mark the pterodactyl's death and leave as soon as they are completed—parallels his recognition that the pterodactyl is beyond his comprehension; although he may "get close" to the people of Pirtha, he can never completely bridge the gap that separates them from one another (140).

The lesson Puran learns in Pirtha, "that even after this deeply investigative analysis he knows nothing, understands nothing," is

one that he directly connects to his unwillingness to build a meaningful relationship with Saraswati: "How much has he . . . seen
and written and come back to his safe room where Saraswati ar-
ranges and dusts his books and sits waiting for the day when Puran
will say 'Come into my room and come into my life,' but even that
Puran has not said" (159–60). Whereas before his encounter with
the pterodactyl he had worried that his solitary personal life might
impair his insights as a journalist, Puran discovers that the opposite is true: unless he can successfully navigate his experiences in
Pirtha, "no justice can be done to himself or Saraswati in the Saraswati affair" (119). Over the course of his stay in Pirtha, Puran frequently recalls conversations with Saraswati, often ones in which
she has offered a perspective surprisingly and illuminatingly different from his own. As his visit draws to a close, Harisharan offers
some friendly advice to Puran, who he recognizes "has changed
so in these few days" (173). "*Man!* Go back. Get married. Return
to normal life," Harisharan recommends, to which Puran replies
with surprising ease, "I'll do that" (185). Although Devi provides
us with little detail, Puran's sudden willingness to marry suggests
a new openness to the perspective that Saraswati represents. No
longer threatened or mystified by Saraswati's difference, Puran
envisions building a relationship across it; transformed by his encounter with the pterodactyl, Puran can no longer "remain a distant spectator anywhere in life" (196).

Stories to Pass On

Like the characters in Morrison's and Devi's fictions, readers
of *Beloved* and "Pterodactyl" confront estranging elements that
defy comprehension; in ways that parallel the exorcisms they depict, therefore, these works ultimately sanction the interpretive

gestures that allow readers to bring the unsettling experience of reading to a satisfying conclusion. Although the mimetic real-ness of the ghosts in these works resists established practices of meaning-making, both Morrison's and Devi's conclusions provide frameworks through which these supernatural events can be ac-commodated in existing schema, and thus potentially mobilized in the world. Perhaps not surprisingly, therefore, both *Beloved* and "Pterodactyl" have inspired powerful and persuasive interpreta-tions, despite their fundamental unyieldingness. These interpreta-tions, I contend, aren't misreadings or transgressions of the works' intent; rather, they respond to the texts' own invitations to direct our attention outward from the incomprehensible encounters they stage—even if doing so entails a selective and imperfect en-gagement with the alterity they embody.

"Pterodactyl" concludes, as I have mentioned, with a surprising postscript in which Devi makes precisely the kind of interpretive gesture that, within the fictional storyworld, Puran has been un-able to carry out: ascribing a meaning to the pterodactyl and its appearance. "In this piece," she writes, "no name—such as Madhya Pradesh or Nagesia—has been used literally. Madhya Pradesh is here India, Nagesia village the entire tribal society. I have delib-erately conflated the ways, rules, and customs of different Austric tribes and groups, and the idea of the ancestral soul is my own. I have merely tried to express my estimation, born of experience, of Indian tribal society, through the myth of the pterodactyl" (196). While certainly disorienting for readers who have turned to the novella expecting an authentic account of tribal culture, this postscript nevertheless executes a clear interpretive maneuver: ac-cording to the author herself, the pterodactyl is a "myth" (not real) and stands in metonymic relationship to "tribal society" more broadly. Vague as this may seem, it's significantly more successful than Puran's attempt to understand the pterodactyl symbolically, and it gives the work's readers a clear path to link this fictional creature to our developing understanding of the nonfictional world the novella depicts.

Morrison's famous ending also works to resolve some of the tensions that have defined the novel up to that point, returning us to the realm of realism by allowing the ghost to fade into obscurity: Beloved's story, we are told, is "not a story to pass on" (290). There is an obvious irony to this statement, coming at the close of a novel that does just what it purports to disavow. Like Devi's postscript, Morrison's conclusion, which seems to point toward the breakdown of narrative communication, actually enables it by resolving—or more accurately, de-emphasizing—some of the text's persistent ambiguities. The troubled and troubling relationship between the past and the present is a central theme in *Beloved*, and as Catherine Romagnolo has suggested, Beloved's appearance creates contradictions and paradoxes in the novel's timeline. (Did Beloved's experience of the Middle Passage in the "dark place" occur before, or after, she lived and died as the daughter of an escaped slave?)[20] Allowing Beloved's story to be forgotten allows us, as readers, to place interpretive weight on the lives of the surviving characters and the narrative arc that makes their story primary as Beloved disappears, literally and figuratively, from view. Concluding with the original family at 124—Sethe, Denver, and Paul D.— the novel suggests that what matters most is their ability to move forward, not the unresolved question of who or what Beloved was or, for that matter, the fate of the child she is carrying. If the novel's emphasis on Beloved's mimetic realness frustrates the work of interpretation, this return to the conventions of realism facilitates the novel's broad circulation; unlike Beloved's story, then, Morrison's novel is quite intentionally a story that can be passed on.

Indeed, as we might suspect, both "Pterodactyl" and *Beloved* do get put into circulation—productively—through readings that are, at least to some degree, strategic. By allowing her fiction to be translated into English, Devi takes clear and intentional steps to make its meaning more portable. As Gayatri Spivak explains in the volume's extensive front matter, the anticipated audience for the English translation of *Imaginary Maps* includes English-speaking readers in both the West and India; within this broader category, she imagines and addresses "the multiculturalist US reader," "the expatriate critic," and "the urban radical academic Indian reader," each of whom inevitably brings distinct interests and expectations to bear on a reading of the text.[21] Although Spivak is characteristically wary of these reading positions and their entailments, Devi engages directly with her readers at a distance.[22] Acknowledging that she "do[es] not know" her Western readers, she nevertheless draws a direct parallel between the oppressed status of indigenous groups in the United States and in India. "In America," Devi writes, "I found such lack of information about the Native Americans. Why should American readers want to know from me about Indian tribals, when they have present-day America?"[23] For American readers, Devi implies, the lesson of her fiction might lie closer to home, in the ongoing oppression and disenfranchisement of Native communities in the United States. But it is America's own history of internal colonization, in turn, that she believes will allow these readers to engage meaningfully with her narrative: "I say to my American readers, see what has been done to them [Native Americans], and you will understand what has been done to the Indian tribals. Everywhere it is the same story."[24] Through such acts of strategic essentialism, which equate the experiences of two very different indigenous communities, Devi allows her own fiction to become meaningful beyond its immediate context.

Although the comparison she draws is certainly reductive, it productively resists the exotifying impulse to which her text, read and interpreted by distant readers, might otherwise be susceptible.

Spivak's theoretical deployment of the novella, too, entails an act of interpretation, and a strategic one, albeit somewhat different from Devi's. For Spivak, Devi's novella exemplifies the dynamics of ethical singularity—and in that sense, my reading of the novella in the context of narrative ethics is directly inspired by hers. But "Pterodactyl" and the other stories in *Imaginary Maps* are also a theoretical springboard for Spivak, an opportunity to meditate on and manifest the incommensurability she locates at the heart of translation, and of literary studies more broadly. Enacting her scholarly commitments, Spivak translates Devi's Bengali source text into English prose that is intentionally distancing—stilted, even—privileging strict fidelity over colloquialism in such a way that readers cannot help but encounter the language of the text as other. My intention, in calling attention to Spivak's intellectual investments as a theorist and translator, is not to undermine those efforts, to which my analysis here is directly indebted. But it is true, nevertheless, that Spivak's translation, no less than Devi's postscript, is a gesture that advances interpretation at the expense of certain features of the reader's encounter with the text.

If the pterodactyl, in Spivak's reading, becomes alterity writ large, we inevitably sacrifice something of the particularism that lends ethical force to Devi's narrative: the imaginative encounter with an impossible creature who really exists within the story-world, and the affective pull of watching that creature suffer and die. This dimension of Devi's novella—the reader's emotional investment in the drama of the pterodactyl's survival and Puran's transformation—is, I would argue, attenuated by the intentional difficulty of the English translation. And it is de-prioritized, as I've

suggested, in any thematic reading—which is, at the most fundamental level, what' Spivak's theorizing carries out. Since, as Jennifer Wenzel points out, "reading Mahasweta [Devi] in English
is, to some degree, reading Spivak,"[25] it is hardly surprising to see
Spivak's intellectual investments and interpretive strategies carried
forward in subsequent critical readings of "Pterodactyl," including both Wenzel's and mine, that engage the work thematically:
for Neil Lazarus, Devi's pterodactyl provides a productive figure
for reflecting on the discipline of postcolonial studies, and Manav
Ratti situates the novella in relation to larger questions about
Third World epistemologies.[26]

   Beloved, too, enters into circulation through interpretations
that, in various ways, make its meanings generalizable beyond the
specific experiences of the family at 124 Bluestone Road. Like the
women who join in *Beloved*'s exorcism, each of whom has her
own motive for participating, readers of Morrison's novel have
found her text hospitable to a wide range of different projects and
investments. It has been situated productively in relation to such
varied literary antecedents as William Faulkner, Mark Twain, and
Nathaniel Hawthorne.[27] Within the context of the African American canon, *Beloved* serves as a powerful touchstone for questions
about the nature of historical memory and slavery's fraught but
central place within that history.[28] It's been read through the
lens of trauma, linked to the practices of oral storytelling and
non-Western historiography, and celebrated for its treatment of
black women's embodied experience.[29] In contrast, popular readers have related to the novel's moving account of individual triumph over adversity, a self-referential reading practice promoted
and exemplified by the book's inclusion in Oprah's Book Club, and
one that, no less than more scholarly approaches, the novel's ending intentionally authorizes.[30] "Brow-ism" notwithstanding, each

of these readings is to some degree selective, and each successfully brings the novel to bear on matters beyond the fictional world it depicts.

While the supernatural phenomena at the center of works like *Beloved* and "Pterodactyl" may be especially unsettling, they ultimately reveal something more fundamental about the relationship of fiction to reality: the features of imagined worlds that make them captivating are precisely those that most stubbornly resist being mobilized through the work of interpretation. As a consequence, these works, like the ones I will consider in the following chapters, negotiate self-consciously between the immersive draw of storytelling and the distancing strategies that, in marking the limits of the fictional encounter, allow it to become meaningful in the wider world. Few of us will ever face the impossible questions of how to feed, bury, or mourn a dinosaur, or how to win forgiveness from or quit ourselves of a vengeful baby ghost. It is the space of interpretive possibility that exists between these narratives and the reality we inhabit that allows us to press them into service as ethical guides.

2

Telling the Traumas of History

In Leslie Marmon Silko's novel *Ceremony*, Tayo's intrusive memories transport him from his quiet life at an isolated sheep camp to the jungles of the Pacific where he fought in World War II, and back further to his lonely childhood as an orphan raised in his aunt's family. For Estha, one of the twin protagonists of Arundhati Roy's *The God of Small Things*, the inky octopus that blots out his memories of the past can never obscure one unforgettable image from his childhood, the broken body of his friend Velutha, beaten to death by the police. For these characters, the past is a haunting presence, one that intrudes into and dramatically alters their lives in the present.

The intrusive memories experienced by Tayo, Estha, and Estha's twin sister, Rahel, have all the hallmarks of psychological trauma, the uncontrollable return of a past experience so troubling that it could not be fully grasped or understood when it occurred. These recurring memories are incredibly vivid but, despite their immediacy and force, resist being fitted into a comprehensible narrative of the past. It's no surprise, therefore, that the effects of trauma are frequently likened in both clinical and theoretical contexts to a form of haunting or possession.[1] Like the ghosts in the previous chapter, the presence of the traumatic past is insistent, troubling, and disruptive, challenging the boundaries between now and then, here and there, real and unreal. But for all its immediacy, the traumatic past, like a ghost, remains opaque and inscrutable, and it is the very incomprehensibility of these past events that causes their uncontrollable return. If, as Cathy Caruth suggests, "to be traumatized is precisely to be possessed by an image or event," trauma throws the claims that the past can make on us into dramatic relief.[2]

Like many works of so-called trauma fiction, *Ceremony* and *The God of Small Things* not only depict characters who experience trauma, but also seemingly enact trauma on the level of narrative form, so that the experience of reading the text mirrors the cognitive processes and affective responses of survivors: time is disjointed, and memories or sense impressions appear without context. In these two novels, in particular, trauma works to make the enduring consequences of imperialism sensible to readers as felt experience, rather than objective knowledge, in ways that can have meaningful ethical consequences. Indeed, the idea that fiction, by simulating the effects of traumatic memory in this way, might induce in its readers the same kinds of powerful and unsettling emotions it sets out to describe is the underlying premise of literary trauma theory. For trauma theorists, who draw an analogy between literary narratives and survivor testimony, this power to collapse the distance between teller and witness, or character and reader, is either trauma's great promise or its great peril. In either case, if we are to take trauma seriously as the source of a narrative ethics, we must think carefully about the question of identification: What's at stake when comparatively privileged readers align themselves with the victimized and the oppressed through the mechanism of literary perspective-taking?

Both of the novels I consider in this chapter are notable for the success with which they invite their readers—including their majoritarian readers—to align themselves with traumatized characters like Tayo, Estha, and Rahel and, by doing so, encourage them to embrace resistant or revisionary narratives of history from below. This kind of sustained perspective-taking is essential to *Ceremony*'s larger political and ideological project, while *The God of Small Things* at some times reproduces the illogic of traumatic memory, but at others relies on its readers' critical distance to supplement its characters' foreshortened vision. But in important ways, I argue, the mediating presence of a third-person narrator in these works complicates models of literary trauma—both those that celebrate traumatic "contagion" as the source of ethical engagement and those that express concern about the dangers of inappropriate identification. Ultimately, I suggest, the ethical impact of these works is attributable not to the uncontrollable disruptions of trauma, but to calculated choices about how to narrate the past.

Traumas of Empire

The critical turn toward affect has solidified our understanding of the ways in which broader structures of political power are enacted on, in, and through the realm of felt experience, and both *Ceremony* and *The God of Small Things* powerfully illustrate how the traumas of empire play themselves out in the intimate and familial relationships between lovers, parents and children, and siblings. As Gregory Seigworth and Melissa Gregg acknowledge in their introduction to the foundational *Affect Theory Reader*, the politically engaged scholarship "undertaken by feminists, queer theorists, disability activists, and subaltern peoples" has long been concerned with "the hard and fast materialities, as well as the fleeting and flowing ephemera" of affective experience.[3] Rather than displacing a critique of the political and social forces that might cause individual suffering, trauma theory makes those forces visible and opens them to interrogation; as Ann Cvetkovich suggests, trauma functions as a "hinge between systemic structures of exploitation and oppression and the felt experience of them."[4] For readers of these two novels, in particular, depictions of trauma bring the human costs of imperial power into sharp focus.

Ceremony tells the story of Tayo, a Native American veteran of the Second World War who has been left shattered by his combat experiences. The illegitimate child of a white father whose identity remains unknown, Tayo is raised by his aunt and remembers very little about his mother, who dies while he is still young. His cousin, Rocky, whom his aunt clearly favors, is a star football player who aspires to lead the assimilated life that is valorized at school. The two young men enlist together, and when Rocky is killed in combat, Tayo feels responsible for his death, as well as for that of his beloved uncle Josiah, who dies while they are away at war. Like many other Native American veterans, Tayo struggles with alcohol abuse, but after he seeks help from Betonie, an unusual Native healer, his perspective changes. According to Betonie, the evils of the modern age, including the arrival of whites in America and the invention of the atom bomb, are the result of Native witchery, which it is Tayo's mission to resist. Following Betonie's advice, Tayo searches for and recovers Josiah's stolen cattle; during his search he meets and begins a romantic relationship with a woman named Ts'eh, who teaches him about traditional forms of healing.[5] Forced into a confrontation with his longtime adversary, Emo, who tortures and kills Tayo's friend Harley, Tayo chooses not to intervene or retaliate and, by doing so, frustrates the witchery's bloodthirsty purpose. At the close of the novel, Tayo no longer suffers from survivor's guilt and traumatic flashbacks and is beginning the process of becoming a Native healer himself.

In Silko's text, the traumas of empire are rooted in uniquely American logics of civilization, modernity, and manifest destiny, shaped not only by the particular history of white racism against indigenous peoples, but also by the resulting concern with cultural preservation and racial purity within Native communities.[6] Although the United States' involvement in World War II is not usually thought of as an instance of colonialism, Silko's treatment of the war emphasizes the connections between Tayo's status as a Native American and the particular traumas of his military service. As Alan Wald has argued, Silko's depiction of Tayo's trauma suggests not only that "similar mechanisms of racism and economic exploitation are involved in *all* wars waged by the United States," but also that "American imperialism's crimes against people of color are not simply aberrations."[7]

As a member of an internally colonized minority, Tayo identifies with the Japanese soldiers he is fighting, who are also framed by U.S. wartime discourse as nationally and ethnically other. The connection that Tayo feels between himself and the Japanese—a connection structured by the operation of U.S. imperialism—is dramatized by his irrational but unshakable conviction that his uncle Josiah is one of the men facing his firing squad during his deployment in the Pacific: "Tayo stood there, stiff with nausea, while they fired at the soldiers, and he watched his uncle fall, and he *knew* it was Josiah; and even after Rocky started shaking him by the shoulders and telling him to stop crying, it was *still* Josiah lying there."[8] Importantly, although Tayo's fellow soldiers dismiss his vision of Josiah as "hallucinations" brought on by "battle fatigue" (8), Betonie later validates Tayo's sense of personal connection with the Japanese soldiers. "It isn't surprising you saw him with them. You saw who they were. Thirty thousand years ago they were not strangers" (124). In a similar moment, at the train depot after

Tayo's release from the veterans' hospital, his traumatic memory transforms a young Japanese American boy in an army hat into his cousin Rocky. The image of the boy blurs the distinctions between Japanese soldiers, Japanese American civilians, and Tayo's own Native American family and sends Tayo into a fit of terrified crying and vomiting. As the novel suggests, there is a germ of truth in Tayo's traumatic visions of Josiah and Rocky: they reveal the shared marginalization and state-sponsored violence experienced by those, such as Japanese Americans and Native Americans, whom nationalist discourse defines as outsiders. In Tayo's mind, military service makes him responsible for the deaths of both his uncle and his cousin, and the guilt he feels about these deaths suggests his profound ambivalence, as a Native American, about his role in the U.S. military.

Tayo's mixed-race identity is also a source of trauma that is shaped by and reflective of imperial power; so much so that, as Naomi Rand points out, Tayo's "home life, and the battles waged there, are indistinguishable from the battle he has fought as a combatant overseas."[9] The novel makes clear that the guilt and shame associated with his mother's promiscuity reflect the Native community's perceived inferiority and embattled cultural identity. His mother, Laura, is herself a victim of this double bind, ashamed both of her culture and of her violation of its norms. The community's judgmental reaction, in turn, masks its dismay at "losing her" and also, therefore, "losing part of themselves" (68). This logic, which equates sexual and cultural purity, also lies just below the surface of Tayo's simmering conflict with Emo, who embraces the values of white society and the sadistic violence of modern war. Like many of the other veterans, Emo acts out his status as a second-class citizen in his sexual relationships, and stories about dancing with blondes and going to bed with redheads while in uniform feature prominently in his drunken reminiscences. When Emo goads Tayo, "You love Japs the way your mother loved to screw white men" (63), he equates Laura's cultural and sexual betrayal with Tayo's betrayal of his country at war: both mother and son are accused of loving the enemy, an accusation that maps the violence of imperialist war onto the terrain of intimate relations. By linking the personal and the political in this way, the novel underscores the fundamental connection between American militarism abroad and racism at home and dramatically illustrates their profound human cost through its depiction of Tayo's physical and psychological suffering.

In a similar way, *The God of Small Things* juxtaposes the smallness of individual lives with the larger political currents that shape, impinge on, and in some cases end them. In Roy's novel, the legacies of British colonialism in India are inseparably intertwined with the competing and sometimes contradictory logics of caste and class privilege, as well as with the specific regional identity of Kerala, which is known for both its significant Christian population and its embrace of Communism. The novel is narrated cyclically, alternating between an account of events that unfold for the novel's protagonists, the twins Estha and Rahel, in December 1969, and their consequences, more than twenty years later, when brother and sister are reunited as adults. The 1969 storyline begins with the arrival of the twins' cousin, Sophie Mol, the daughter of their uncle, Chacko, and his British ex-wife, Margaret Kochamma. During Margaret Kochamma's and Sophie Mol's visit, the twins' mother, Ammu, begins an affair with Velutha, an Untouchable carpenter, that sets off a chain reaction of tragic events that includes Sophie Mol's accidental drowning; Velutha's arrest on false kidnapping charges, which the twins are coerced into corroborating; and Velutha's fatal beating by the police, which the twins witness. In the aftermath of these events, Ammu is separated from her children, forced to leave her family's home, becomes impoverished and ill, and eventually dies. Estha is "Returned" to his father,[10] while Rahel remains in Ayemenem to be raised by her uncle; both twins endure loveless childhoods and, as adults, lead hollow lives haunted by the past.

For the twins, the past is a malign and persistent presence, and the recurring image of the "History House" exemplifies this understanding of history as, in the words of Anuradha Dingwaney Needham, "a dominating, oppressive force that saturates virtually all social and cultural space, including familial, intimate, and affective relationships."[11] The phrase is coined by Chacko, who likens history to "an old house at night. With all the lamps lit. And ancestors whispering inside" (51). As he explains to the twins, the legacies of British imperialism have left them, as former colonial subjects, "pointed in the wrong direction, trapped outside their own history," like people viewing a house from the outside (51). For the children, this explanation makes sense immediately: they know a house like the one Chacko describes, the abandoned estate of Kari Saipu, an Englishman "gone native," that is located across the river from their home (51). Kari Saipu's house, the twins' History House, has a sordid past, standing vacant after its owner committed suicide when his underage Indian lover was taken from him and sent to school. The History House, then, like the twins' own family, is haunted by the specter of imperial power and the forms of violence and exploitation it authorizes: Vellya Paapen, the family's servant, reports that Kari Saipu's ghost still haunts the property, pleading with deceptive gentility for the cigar that will magically free him from his captivity.

Indeed, the family's staunch Anglophilia, which Chacko freely acknowledges (he makes the twins look up the word), is a manifestation of India's colonial past that is inseparable from their often fraught personal relationships. Pappachi, the twins' cruel and abusive grandfather, is, in Ammu's words, "an incurable British CCP," or "shit-wiper" (50). The intimate lives of both of Pappachi's children, Ammu and Chacko, are in turn marked by the legacies of British colonialism: Ammu's marriage to her abusive, alcoholic husband disintegrates after he proposes that she become the mistress of his British supervisor, and when she returns to her parents' home in disgrace as a young divorcée, Pappachi rejects her story because he refuses to believe that "an Englishman, *any* Englishman, would covet another man's wife" (42). Chacko, a Rhodes scholar who prides himself on his time spent at Oxford, is attracted to his white, British ex-wife's freckles and continues to adore her after their divorce in part because he sees himself as so unworthy of her. And the twins, yearning for a father figure, measure themselves heartbreakingly against the "clean, white children" in *The Sound of Music*, only to be rejected in their own imaginations by Baron von Trapp (100). The twins' sense of rejection, like Ammu's "Unsafe Edge" and Chacko's heartbreak (44), is a form of trauma reflecting the legacies of imperialism, alive and well in the present.

The central event of the novel, Velutha's fatal beating, powerfully demonstrates the embodied, personal cost of abstractions such as "human nature's pursuit of ascendancy" and "power's fear of powerlessness" (292–93). In this climactic scene, all of the political currents and personal motives that Roy has traced throughout the novel converge. The ingrained prejudice of the twins' grandmother, Mammachi, raises the stakes when she learns of her daughter's affair with Velutha, and her grudging tolerance of Chacko's dalliances fuels her disgust at Ammu for "defil[ing] generations of breeding" (244). A recent Communist march inspires anger, fear, and humiliation in Baby Kochamma, the twins' lonely, bitter great-aunt, which she projects onto Velutha in her false police report. The death of Sophie Mol, a "clean, white" British child, makes the alleged kidnapping all the more shocking to the authorities, who react accordingly. The high-caste policemen, acting as "history's henchmen," beat Velutha with brutal efficiency, his ruined body the product of "an era imprinting itself on those who lived in it" (292, 293). And finally, as Velutha lies dying in the police station, Baby Kochamma uses the twins' love for their mother and for each other to coerce the false identification that corroborates her report and justifies "the Death in Custody of a technically innocent man" (298).

In both novels, trauma makes visible the embodied, human cost of imperialism in characters' lives. As a means of engaging the broad, majoritarian audiences to which, at least in part, these works are addressed, focusing on the intimate and the affective is an approach that renders abstract political structures concrete and relatable. Despite the skepticism of commentators like Aijaz Ahmad, who objects that Roy's novel "dismisses the actually constituted field of politics as either irrelevant or a zone of bad faith," the strategy of making the political personal is so common in ethnic and Third World literature as to seem almost de rigueur.[12] In many foundational texts, the turn to the personal is a powerful authorizing move, creating a terrain from which marginalized writers can safely push back against structures of oppression in which their readers may well be complicit—think, for instance, of works like *Things Fall Apart*, *Nervous Conditions*, or *The Bluest Eye*. It makes good sense to connect with distant and potentially resistant readers on the basis of such supposedly apolitical shared experiences, and showing how they are contaminated by entrenched forms of oppression can poignantly illustrate the damage done by abstract political structures. In both *Ceremony* and

The God of Small Things, this effect is intensified by formal strategies that reproduce the effects of trauma and, by doing so, invite
readers to take on the altered, potentially resistant perspectives of
their traumatized protagonists. This has, indeed, been the basis for
many of the claims made about these works' resistant politics. As
I will suggest, however, a closer examination of the formal properties of so-called traumatic narrative suggests that the relationship
between traumatic style and revisionary history is more complex
and fraught than it might initially appear.

Traumatic Form and the Question of Contagion

Storytelling—in particular, the survivor's ability or inability to integrate the events of his or her life into a comprehensible
narrative—is essential to clinical understandings of trauma and
recovery.[13] Indeed, through a certain lens, the primary difference
between narratives that reproduce trauma and narratives that
heal it can be seen as a difference in form: the language of trauma
is disjointed, interruptive, and repetitive, whereas a healing narrative is linear and integral; the intrusions of trauma are experienced in the present tense, whereas a healing narrative confines the
causative events to the past. More than simply describing trauma,
therefore, *Ceremony* and *The God of Small Things* can be said to
reproduce it through formal strategies such as fragmentation and
repetition that generate a reading experience not unlike the experience of traumatic memory. Inviting character identification and
perspective-taking in this way is a particularly powerful strategy for
authors like Silko and Roy, whose fictions are written, at least in part,
with cultural outsiders in mind—nonindigenous readers in Silko's
case, and international readers in Roy's.[14] Assuming the perspective of traumatized characters like Tayo or the twins, which refuses

order, logic, and objectivity, not only collapses social distance but also fundamentally alters our relationship, as readers, to the historical past and the structures of power it inscribes. This is what foundational trauma theorist Cathy Caruth sees as both the artistic and the ethical potential of traumatic narrative: it reconfigures our understanding of the world around us in ways that can put us, as readers, in solidarity with the victimized and the oppressed.

Both *Ceremony* and *The God of Small Things* share many of the hallmarks of traumatic narrative; that is, they employ formal features and narrative strategies that seem to mirror the cognitive and affective experience of trauma survivors.[15] Perhaps most prominently, both novels are narrated nonlinearly, providing information about the past in fragmentary and disjointed snippets, often without the context necessary to make them meaningful. *Ceremony* begins with Tayo, recently returned from the war, living at his family's remote sheep camp; scenes from his present alternate with vivid depictions of the Pacific jungles where he saw combat and with childhood memories of time spent with Rocky and Josiah. These scenes interrupt the narration of present events as completely and as forcefully as the memories themselves intrude on Tayo's consciousness; just as Tayo is incapacitated by these involuntary flashbacks, it takes almost fifty pages for Silko to narrate Tayo's journey from the sheep camp to the bar, so densely are these pages filled with detailed depictions of scenes from his past.

The God of Small Things, too, is narrated as if through traumatic flashbacks, beginning with Estha's and Rahel's return to Ayemenem as adults and moving by association backward into the past. Key events are narrated out of sequence: in the first chapter, we witness Sophie Mol's funeral without knowing the cause of her death, and we're told about Estha being "Returned" to his father before learning of the events that led to his being separated from his mother and sister (12). The novel's narrator even comments explicitly on the difficulty of shaping the twins' lives into a story with a clear beginning, middle, and end: suggesting that the question of when "it all began" remains open to debate, the narrator considers a number of possibilities before establishing the family's trip to Cochin in 1969 as the story's starting point merely "for practical purposes, in a hopelessly practical world" (32, 34).

Another feature of traumatic memory is the way it distorts both the duration and intensity of certain memories: often, the sensory attributes of a traumatic event are recorded in the survivor's mind with incredible detail and immediacy. In the context of a literary narrative, this quality of traumatic memory alters the rules of notice and signification that determine which narrative elements readers are likely to attend to. As Peter Rabinowitz has observed, the rules determining what features of a narrative are significant, like many other elements of readers' engagements with texts, are governed by convention.[16] So in the context of a major event like Rocky's death or Velutha's beating, sense imagery like the crunching sounds on which Tayo fixates, or the scent of "old roses on a breeze" that Rahel discerns (8), might seem to be merely devices of literary figuration and be overlooked. Repeating these images out of context, however, not only captures a character's feeling of being possessed by an intrusive, visceral memory (the crushing of Rocky's skull, or the smell of Velutha's blood), but also ensures that readers notice them and recognize their significance. In this way, too, readers are encouraged to adopt a perspective that, like that of the characters, is often radically foreshortened.

Such a perspective, shaped by trauma, reveals that, in making sense of stories like Tayo's or the twins', the "facts," established with the benefit of critical distance, are often not the most important. Rather, it's in the seemingly insignificant details that both characters and readers can locate the possibility of an alternate or even resistant narrative. For Tayo, details like the colors of plants or clouds reveal the pattern underlying his incomprehensible experiences—the workings of the destroyers—and provide him with the necessary tools and knowledge to heal both himself and society at large. In Roy's novel, the titular God of Small Things personifies all that which, both good and bad, is dwarfed by conflicts and tragedies on a national and international scale. Although Small God comes away from his encounter with Big God "cauterized, laughing numbly at his own temerity [and] inured by the confirmation of his own inconsequence" (20), he is also responsible for the small pleasures that make characters' lives bearable: the humble insects that Ammu and Velutha fret over together, and "the disconnected delights of underwater farting" that the twins relish (194).

For trauma theorists like Caruth, then, the power of traumatic narrative lies in the particular way it invites—or even requires—its readers to take on the fragmented, distorted perspective of traumatized characters, likening the reader of fiction to the witness of a survivor's testimony. Fictional narratives, like the narratives of trauma survivors, have a rhetorical dimension: they are stories told to someone, for a particular purpose.[17] In clinical settings, the presence of a witness is central to the process of producing a healing narrative of traumatic events, because the witness's willingness to listen is what allows the survivor to reconstruct a story of his or her experience. Such witnessing, however, brings with it the risk of "contagion": the witness identifies so strongly with the survivor that he or she, in turn, becomes traumatized and suffers from the same intrusive images or feelings of powerlessness.[18] For therapists like Judith Herman, this is a risk inherent in the process of working with trauma survivors in a clinical setting: at times, she explains, the therapist becomes "emotionally overwhelmed" and "experiences, to a lesser degree, the same terror, rage, and despair as the patient."[19] In a literary rather than a clinical context, however, the idea that a traumatic narrative has the power to impose itself involuntarily on a witness can have more positive implications. Trauma theorists often identify traumatic contagion as a constructive mechanism by which a work of fiction might be able to act on and change its readers—in other words, as the source of trauma fiction's unique ethical force.

Along these lines, Caruth argues that traumatic memory exists, like literary fiction itself, outside of the realm of objective knowledge, and this nonreferential quality—what she calls trauma's "impossibility"—demands a fundamentally different kind of listening. "To be able to listen to the impossible," she writes, "is also to have been *chosen* by it, *before* the possibility of mastering it with knowledge."[20] Witnesses, she implies, are already a lot like readers of fiction, who allow themselves to be moved by stories that, although not necessarily factual, they experience as emotionally true. For Caruth, then, contagion becomes a powerful mechanism of interpellation, the source of "trauma's address beyond itself."[21] In this model, traumatic narrative collapses the distance between survivor and witness, text and reader, in ways that echo the logic of haunting: stories of trauma demand to be heard, and by hearing them, in all their resistance to order and logic, we subject ourselves to their demands. Not surprisingly, therefore, Caruth suggests that trauma, by staging encounters with otherness, has the potential to bridge cultural divides: "In a catastrophic age," she contends, "trauma itself may provide the very link between cultures: not as simple understanding of the pasts of others but rather, within the traumas of contemporary history, as our ability to listen through the departures we have all taken from ourselves."[22]

The model Caruth proposes—in which traumatic narrative has the power to traverse boundaries of difference and thereby transform its readers—is one that *Ceremony*, in particular, seems to validate. As the novel makes clear, stories are ceremonies, and telling them has the potential to change not just their tellers, but their listeners as well. The novel opens with an account of the mythic figure Ts'its'tsi'nako, or Thought-Woman, who has the ability to bring stories to life; as the narrator of this prologue explains, Ts'its'tsi'nako is thinking of a story, and "whatever she thinks about / appears" (1). When the narrator then declares, directly addressing the novel's readers, "I'm telling you the story / she is thinking" (1), the novel itself becomes one of Ts'its'tsi'nako's stories, which, through its telling, becomes real. As Robert Bell, among others, has suggested, the story of Ts'its'tsi'nako can be seen as part of a curative ritual with the power to affect the world through its very repetition.[23] By participating in the kind of transformative storytelling that Silko's novel carries out, the prologue seems to suggest, we ourselves become participants in the healing ceremony that it stages.

Indeed, in a common interpretation of *Ceremony*, the novel guides its readers through a healing ceremony in which not only Tayo, but they themselves are included.[24] At the start of the novel, readers likely experience the novel's interruptive, nonlinear narration as disorienting or even frustrating since, like Tayo, we are bombarded with information and images but denied the perspective needed to make sense of them. The traumatic style of narration prevalent toward the beginning of the novel gradually becomes more linear and grounded in the present after Tayo's visit to Betonie, when his quest to recover Josiah's stolen cattle and defeat the witchery provides structure, sequence, and meaning to his previously shattered life. In this latter section of the novel, Tayo's memories inform rather than interrupt his decisions and actions in the present, as when, during his search for the cattle, he remembers the lessons learned from childhood hunting trips with Rocky and Josiah. For the reader, too, this section provides a sense of calm and relief. After the struggle of reconstructing Tayo's story in the novel's early pages, we are now able to follow a clear and purposeful sequence of events—indeed, the familiar plot of a quest or adventure—to its clear and logical conclusion.

By constructing a narrative that aligns its readers with Tayo in this way, *Ceremony* also encourages us, implicitly, to embrace the concept of witchery's pervasive and pernicious influence on the modern world, since it is by accepting Betonie's alternate history that Tayo is able to begin the process of healing. According to Betonie, the violence and cruelty of modernity, including the arrival of whites in America, the genocide of Native Americans, and the carnage of modern war, can be attributed to the work of Native witches, the destroyers. He reassures Tayo that although whites might seem to be the cause of Indians' suffering, "white people are only tools that the witchery manipulates; and I tell you, we can deal with white people, with their machines and their beliefs. We can because we invented white people; it was Indian witchery that made white people in the first place" (132). For readers of the novel, Betonie's account of history is tantalizing, for it reframes the history of European colonization, and Native communities' consequent displacement and disenfranchisement, in terms that make Native Americans agents rather than victims, much as a survivor's healing narrative might. If Native witches are the cause of the destruction that Tayo and Betonie witness in the world around them, then they and others like them also have the power to stop that destruction and frustrate the witchery's plans.

Crucially, the logic of Betonie's alternate history is not only essential to Tayo's process of healing, but also shapes the novel's larger narrative arc and is central to understanding the climactic contest between Tayo and Emo. Given both the means and the motive to confront and kill the sadistic Emo, Tayo chooses not to intervene and watches passively while Emo tortures and kills his friend Harley. In the terms of the conventional Western hero plot, Tayo's choice would be seen as cowardly, for he has failed to show loyalty by protecting his friend. In the context of Silko's novel, however, this scene is presented as a triumph, because by resisting the trap set for him by Emo and refusing to meet violence with violence, Tayo ruins the destroyers' evil ritual. In order to read this scene as the climax of the plot and the culmination of Tayo's personal development, as the novel's structure invites us to do, we must accept the alternate history of the witchery that justifies Tayo's actions as heroic rather than cowardly. For the novel to conclude with the satisfying experience of Tayo's success, we must accept the notion of the witchery and embrace the struggle to defeat it as the novel's central dynamic. This scene is one of several moments in which, as Sean Kicummah Teuton has argued, "Silko carefully inserts tribal experience so that mainstream readers must rely on these supernatural experiences to understand the text and to value their universal appeal to overturn destructive worldviews."[25]

Aligning our perspective with Tayo in this way, however, positions the novel's readers—including its non-Native readers—among the victims of witchery who might benefit from the kind of curative ceremony the novel enacts. Although Betonie's inversion of the received narrative of American history, in which European settlers are the creation of Native sorcerers, recenters Native Americans in the story of their own past, it also allows the novel's white readers to occupy a comfortable place in that story: rather than being the perpetrators or beneficiaries of history's traumas, white readers are, like Tayo, among its victims. In fact, in the model that the novel offers, white privilege becomes the corollary of Native shame: both are pernicious consequences of the witchery's malignant design.[26] The question of *Ceremony*'s address to its non-Native readers is an important one, since, as Allan Chavkin has pointed out, more than half a million copies of the novel were sold in the two decades following its initial publication, and by the early 2000s it had become "one of the most frequently taught contemporary novels in higher education."[27] Given these statistics, we can safely assume that the novel has had many white readers—perhaps even a disproportionate number, judging by the continuing underrepresentation of minority students in America's colleges and universities. How it positions those white readers is, then, a matter of some consequence.

Indeed, the very quality some critics praise in the novel—its broadly inclusive address to both Native and non-Native readers—is troubling to others, who see it as a violation of cultural norms. Among its admirers, Carol Mitchell celebrates the novel's blending of old and new forms, which she hopes will "help to cure some of the hopelessness and despair of the contemporary Indian who is caught between two ways of life."[28] James Ruppert similarly praises what he terms the novel's "mediational" quality; by combining Native and non-Native epistemologies, he argues, the novel is able to "restructure how each audience [Native and non-Native] values truth, reality, and knowledge."[29] Others, however, express reservations about that very same hybridizing impulse and are critical of Silko's willingness to share sacred stories with non-Native audiences. Jana Sequoya-Magdaleno, for instance, takes issue with the way the novel's prologue invites both Laguna and Western reading practices, which she argues are mutually exclusive.[30] And Paula Gunn Allen, a noted critic of the novel, impugns Silko for revealing sacred stories to uninitiated audiences; she speculates, pointedly, that Silko "must have been told what I was, that we don't tell these things outside."[31] Significantly, none of these differing responses to the novel questions the effectiveness of its gestures of interpellation; they do, however, suggest the ethical complexities that attend the forms of perspective-taking and alignment that the novel invites.

Silko's critics are hardly alone in recognizing the risk of appropriation involved in narrating the traumatic past; in fact, what Caruth identifies as trauma's power to bridge across differences, historian Dominick LaCapra sees as one of its perils. Although he affirms a view of historical inquiry "wherein knowledge involves not only the processing of information but also affect, empathy, and questions of value," LaCapra cautions that an inappropriate identification with survivors of trauma risks absolving witnesses of their obligation to account for the events of the past, and might lead them to disregard the distinct "ethical, social, and political demands and responsibilities" that attend their "relative good fortune."[32] He writes, "If we who have not been severely traumatized by experiences involving massive losses go to the extreme of identifying (however spectrally or theoretically) with the victim and survivor, our horizon may unjustifiably become that of the survivor . . . at least as we imagine her or him to be."[33] For LaCapra, as for Sequoya-Magdaleno and Allen, questions of positionality matter, and forms of empathetic engagement that elide these differences may undermine, rather than engender, ethical responsibility.

In the case of *Ceremony*, then, the novel's non-Native readers might be involved in precisely the kind of inappropriate identification that LaCapra describes. On the one hand, a narrative that places blame squarely on white America for social ills like Native poverty, alcoholism, and ingrained perceptions of racial and cultural inferiority can be disempowering. This is, in essence, Emo's way of thinking: taking for granted that whites have claimed for themselves everything worth having, Emo recognizes his oppression but reifies the logic by which Native land, Native culture, and Native women are inferior to their white counterparts. As the novel suggests, this is a profoundly destructive mindset for characters like Tayo and the other Native veterans, and Tayo's embrace of an alternate narrative is what allows him to form nourishing and sustaining relationships with his family, his culture, and the natural world around him. But from a different perspective, it is essential that non-Native readers recognize the truth behind Emo's story, and their potential complicity in it—including the ways in which they may have benefited, directly or indirectly, from the expropriation of Native lands, and the ways in which such economic and social benefits are passed down for generations. The risk that LaCapra discerns is that, by aligning themselves too completely with history's victims, majoritarian readers might be all too ready to efface their own complicity in historical acts of violence and domination.

To a greater extent than *Ceremony*, *The God of Small Things* underscores the ethical problems that can emerge from inappropriate or excessive identification with history's victims—the kind of "participatory or emulative relation" to the traumatic past that LaCapra warns may inhibit our ability to think critically about history.[34] The example of the History House, Kari Saipu's abandoned estate, provides one such cautionary tale. Years after the novel's main events, the History House, the site of Velutha's fatal beating, is transformed into a resort called "Heritage." At Heritage, the resort owners create "toy Histories for rich tourists to play in" by relocating the ancestral homes of local families and positioning them around Kari Saipu's home "in attitudes of deference" that evoke an idealized—and entirely fabricated—colonial past (120).

The truncated kathakali performances that take place there, shortened to cater to the "imported attention spans" of its guests, make a mockery of the epic stories of India's past that the full dances convey (220). As Roy makes bitingly clear, the alternate narrative peddled by Heritage appeals to its guests precisely because it effaces their complicity in colonialism, class oppression, and caste oppression, much as the hotel itself seeks to conceal the poverty and pollution that surround it, unpleasant realities for which its patrons share responsibility. By layering the present-day activities of the resort over the physical traces of what happened there years before, like Rahel's abandoned wristwatch, the novel cautions its readers against accepting such self-serving and inaccurate accounts of the past; we know the History House's brutal past, even if its current residents prefer to forget it.

For Estha and Rahel, too, fidelity to the past is an ethical imperative, even though it comes at great personal cost. As adults, the twins continue to suffer from the trauma they experienced as children: Estha has chosen to stop speaking; and Rahel, whose distant, vacant eyes offend her ex-husband during their lovemaking, is left empty by all that she has lost. Despite their evident pain, however, the twins remain unwilling or unable to construct a healing narrative; to do so, as the narrator suggests—to "purchase, for a fee, some cheap brand of exorcism from a counselor with a fancy degree"— seems to them a self-serving betrayal of the past: "It would have helped if they could have made that crossing. If only they could have worn, even temporarily, the tragic hood of victimhood. Then they would have been able to put a face on it, and conjure up fury at what had happened. Or seek redress. And eventually, perhaps, exorcise the memories that haunted them. But this anger wasn't available to them. . . . Esthappen and Rahel both knew that there were several perpetrators (besides themselves) that day. But only one victim" (182). An explicit rejection of the sort of revisionary narratives that allow trauma survivors to "exorcise the memories that haun[t] them," this passage insists that the twins share some culpability for their role in Velutha's death, which a responsible account of the past cannot ignore. By emphasizing the twins' resistance to claiming a victimhood that, to their minds, they do not deserve, Roy indirectly but clearly challenges the analogous desire her readers might feel to identify—perhaps inappropriately—with the suffering of characters like Estha and Rahel.

At the same time, however, the absolutism of this passage may chafe against readers' own empathetic sentiments, artfully elicited in the novel's preceding pages. By filtering its account through the childlike perspective of the twins, the novel allows its readers to experience a horror at events like Velutha's death that, in the broader context of world affairs, might seem insignificant. We also share the twins' recognition, as adults, of their relative privilege within the class and caste systems that shaped those events. But in moments such as this, I would argue, our alignment with their perspective wavers. Although Estha and Rahel may not be able to see themselves as two victims among many, the novel's readers, who have observed their often uncomprehending participation in the machinations of the adults around them, have strong reasons to be more forgiving. A passage such as this one, I believe, invites readers not to identify with Estha and Rahel, but instead, to adopt a more distant, rational perspective that remains inaccessible to the twins and that allows us to recognize them as more "Sinned Against" than "Sinners" (182).

This distancing effect illustrates another important difference between *Ceremony* and *The God of Small Things*. The political intervention that Silko stages relies on readers' successful and persistent alignment with her characters, which is underwritten by the novel's narrative structure. *Ceremony* invites its readers to embrace an alternate narrative of American history that overturns established facts and relies on Native thought and belief systems about the supernatural power of witchery and the fundamental interconnectedness of the world. This transformative shift in perception is supported by the kind of perspective-taking that the novel encourages, which aligns readers with Tayo and rewards them with the effect of coherence and catharsis. Without this alignment, such transformative effects aren't possible; if readers distance themselves from Tayo, as my students sometimes do, the novel becomes merely a quaint story about someone else's beliefs, with little power or bearing on their own lives.

The God of Small Things asks something importantly different of its readers. In contrast to *Ceremony*, in which Tayo possesses the unifying narrative of empire and resistance that readers are encouraged to embrace, the politics of Roy's novel depend on its readers' ability to see the bigger picture in ways that its characters cannot. The case of Chacko's model airplanes perfectly illustrates the particular kind of double vision that the novel's narrative perspective both enables and relies on for its political critique. Month after month, Chacko eagerly anticipates the arrival of a model airplane kit, and he builds the planes with gusto, even though they invariably crash: "Chacko's room was cluttered with broken wooden planes. And every month another kit would arrive. Chacko never blamed the crashes on the kit" (55). The novel's third-person narrator offers us a perspective unavailable to Chacko, who lacks the insight to blame the kit, as we are prompted to do. The airplane kit exemplifies the dynamics at work throughout the world of the novel, in which so many characters, like Chacko, are working within flawed systems at projects doomed to failure. What Roy offers us, and what her characters importantly lack, is the impetus and the necessary perspective to carry out this kind of structural critique.

Unlike *Ceremony*, therefore, *The God of Small Things* invites its readers to adopt its characters' restricted perspectives in some moments, while in others, allows us to take a broader view of the social system within which these characters must operate, but which they themselves often fail to discern. Striking this balance is important and necessary in a world where so many of these characters are, as a result of the intersecting systems of religion, politics, caste, class, gender, and empire, both victims and perpetrators. Chacko, for instance, is both a male chauvinist and petty domestic tyrant, on the one hand, and a colonial subject whose "dreams have been doctored" by the logic of the colonizer (52), on the other. In fact, it is Chacko himself who describes the family, inheritors of British colonial ideologies, as victims "of a war that has made us adore our conquerors and despise ourselves" (52). Even as he attempts to provide the twins with this illuminating "Historical Perspective," however, the narrator foreshadows the fact that "Perspective was something which, in the weeks to follow, Chacko himself would sorely lack" (52). Blinded by love and grief, and with no check on his patriarchal power within the household, Chacko lashes out against Ammu and her children after Sophie Mol's death, and as a result is directly responsible for both the children's solitary, loveless upbringing and Ammu's premature death. What Chacko cannot see—the intersecting forms of privilege and subordination that make him both perpetrator and victim—the novel's narrator calls into sharp relief. This is a crucial aspect of the novel's ethical stance, making visible the structures of power that shape the lives of these characters without denying their agency and their culpability in the tragic events of 1969. And it is an ethical stance that depends on readers' ability to distance themselves from characters, at least to some degree.

This subtle but important difference in the ways that *Ceremony* and *The God of Small Things* position their readers brings the question of narration into sharper focus: both novels tell their stories by means of a third-person narrator located outside the diegetic world of the text. Literary trauma theory, analogizing between fictional text and survivor narrative, frequently fails to attend to this dimension of literary storytelling. This raises a crucial question: If the reader of trauma fiction takes on the role of the witness—with all the ethical possibilities and risks that entails—who exactly is the victim? It can't be the author; to assume so would violate the foundational premise of contemporary literary criticism that distinguishes the author's biography from the artistic work he or she has created.[35] And it's not quite the characters, either, though that might be our immediate and intuitive response. Because neither *Ceremony* nor *The God of Small Things* is narrated in the first person, the voice that speaks trauma, in Caruth's locution, is not the voice of Tayo, or Rahel, but rather the mediating voice of a third-person narrator. This is a crucial distinction. Third-person narration implies the presence of a persona (if not a person) that stands apart from the instances of trauma these works depict. And while a trauma survivor's narrative may be fragmentary and imagistic by necessity, a narrator's is so by choice. Recognizing that the accounts of trauma in these works are delivered to us by narrators, rather than characters, means that the disruptive features of the narratives they provide—the disjointed timeline and foreshortened perspective—are not psychological symptoms, but rather aesthetic effects.

In fact, careful attention to the third-person narration in *The God of Small Things* reveals a remarkably complex and fluid manipulation of narrative time and perspective that is fundamentally irreducible to an individual character's traumatic perception. Throughout the novel, the particular lyrical quality of Roy's writing reproduces a child's view of the wonders and mysteries of the adult world: the frequent capitalizations ("Love Laws," 33; "Necessary Politics," 15; "Those with Nothing Up Their Noses," 126) and concatenations ("dustgreen trees," 3; "the Orangedrink Lemondrink man," 5) suggest a childlike impulse to particularize, a resistance to generalization and abstraction that continues to define the novel's narration, even from the vantage of the narrative present, when the twins have become adults. To some extent, this effect can be explained as a mimetic rendering of the twins' traumatic perception, which remains frozen in the past. But this exercise in perspective-taking breaks down at notable moments. When the narrator reports dialogue, for instance, readers expect it to be reported truthfully and completely, as convention dictates, without the limitations of the twins' first-person perspective. Accordingly, when Rahel has stepped away from the "Play" being staged to welcome her aunt and cousin and hidden herself in the airport curtains, the third-person narrator renders the dialogue among the adults in this scene in full (139). What, then, are we to make of the fact that Chacko introduces his sister to his ex-wife as "Ammu, my sister" (137), when "Ammu," in Malayalam, means "mother"? The conceit by which the narrator's use of family titles seems to reflect the point of view of the twins (Ammu is their mother), breaks down in this moment, since Chacko's statement makes no sense from any character's perspective; its implausibility calls attention to the narrator's apparent intervention in recording and recounting the events of the novel.

Similarly, though the disruptions in narrative time may echo the twins' experience of being trapped forever in the past, the emotional effect of the novel's ending, in particular, depends on the narrator's choice to tell the story out of sequence. Rather than concluding with its account of the twins' damaged lives and fraught reconciliation in the present, the novel ends with a flashback to

Ammu and Velutha's lovemaking. Certainly, the novel's rendering of these scenes is bittersweet; by this point, readers know just how much the lovers' stolen moments together will cost them. Nevertheless, ending the novel with an account of their tenderness, mutuality, and the small promise of "tomorrow" (321) does much to counteract the sadness of the story as a whole. This ending, I would argue, reinforces the novel's larger contention that, in the face of overwhelming injustices, the small spaces within individual lives hold the promise of resistance. By completing this thematic arc, it provides readers with a sense of closure that is both politically and ethically significant and, to some degree, pleasurable. And because the twins did not directly witness these love scenes between Ammu and Velutha, we infer that they are being reported to us directly by the narrator; in other words, the twins' traumatic memory is not responsible for this manipulation of narrative time.

If, as I'm suggesting, telling the story out of sequence is what enables the novel's emotional and political appeals to be successful, it is important to recognize that trauma, as such, is not responsible for this effect. The underlying assumption of Caruth's model is that traumatic narrative is authentic, uncensored, a voice from the margins speaking back against History as told by its victors. In the case of a third-person narrative like Roy's, however, this equation of narrative voice with marginalized social locations or subordinated historical actors oversimplifies the relationship between reader and text and potentially misconstrues the nature of its ethical significance. If Roy's novel, and in particular its ending, engages readers in constructing resistant narratives in ways that have ethical implications, it is not because we have been unsettled and transformed by a survivor's testimony. The novel's nonlinear narration, for all its transformative power, is not the voice of trauma speaking from beyond the reach of rational meaning-making; it is the result of a conscious choice about how it is most expedient and productive to narrate the past.

Similarly, it makes sense to consider the role that *Ceremony*'s third-person narration plays in that novel's more capacious address to its readers. Most of the time, *Ceremony*'s third-person narration is more conventionally reliable and self-effacing than Roy's, largely focalized by Tayo or, in a few instances, by other Native American characters, like Helen Jean or the unnamed homeless boy in Gallup, who also experience the traumas of empire firsthand. Nevertheless, the narrator of *Ceremony* occasionally speaks directly to the novel's readers—as when, for instance, the narrator of the prologue introduces Ts'its'tsi'nako and explains that "I'm telling you the story / she is thinking" (1). Moreover, the novel's collage-like structure interweaves Tayo's story with Laguna myths and fables and stylized renderings of Native veterans' oral narratives, suggesting that the novel might have multiple narrators, and even multiple audiences and rhetorical contexts. Indeed, the novel ends with a prayer to the sun ("Sunrise, accept this offering," 262); in one sense then, it is a story told to the sun, as an offering, by someone who worships it. Rather than a narrative persona like that in *The God of Small Things*, who controls and shapes the story, *Ceremony* offers us a multifarious or even collective narrator or narrators, and seems to contain a range of differently structured and directed narrative acts.

Readers of *Ceremony* who embrace its non-Western epistemological practices thus become, in effect, part of the community of listeners entrusted with the perpetuation of powerful clan stories, in ways that might fundamentally alter their relationship to the historical past. This is also not the voice of trauma. To the contrary, what transforms Tayo's perspective is a Native worldview that displaces the medicalized discourse of trauma. In fact, the novel is consistently critical of Western psychology: the veterans' hospital is a place where Tayo loses himself in the drift of "white smoke," and admittance there holds no promise of healing for him (17). One might even argue that reading Tayo's experience through the medicalized discourse of trauma goes against the grain of the novel's invitation to its readers. The kind of storytelling that heals Tayo is communal, continuous, and performative, in the sense of Ts'its'tsi'nako's story, the telling of which is itself an act of creation; we've been successfully interpellated by that narrative only at the moment when we cease to see it as pathological, altered, or revisionary.

While trauma theorists are right to recognize the rhetorical and political power of certain acts of perspective-taking, both *Ceremony* and *The God of Small Things* suggest that our ethical relationship to the past is, by necessity, far more complex than simple identification with history's victims. The effectiveness of the narrative art by which these works draw their readers in can tempt us, as critics, to lose track of their status as consciously and strategically constructed narratives. We *feel as if* we feel with Tayo, and with Estha and Rahel, and the sense of direct, visceral connection to a human being in pain underwrites both novels' very different enactments of anti-imperialist critique. The success of this affective appeal, however, lies not in these works' authenticity as disruptive, irrepressible voices from the margins, but rather in their mediation—the artfulness with which they execute this effect of proximity. Literary depictions of trauma make their readers feel the enduring presence of the past, much as the survivors of imperial violence continue to do. But just as traumatic memory is distinct from the past events that inspired it, fictionalizing trauma is a narrative act with its own ghostly remainder—the past itself is always there, just out of reach.

3

Invisible Victims, Visible Absences

D isappearance is a form of political violence that attempts to erase an individual from the social and political worlds he or she inhabited, leaving behind a ghostly remainder that stubbornly eludes representation. The human rights organization Amnesty International defines the disappeared as "people who have been taken into custody by agents of the state, yet whose whereabouts and fate are concealed, and whose custody is denied."[1] The violence of disappearance is both physical and epistemic: victims are often arrested without notice and detained in secret facilities; few reappear to tell their stories; and if they are killed, their remains are disposed of anonymously. The "disappeared person" is thus a figure defined, first and foremost, by his or her invisibility as a victim.

Not surprisingly, efforts to advocate for the disappeared frequently center around making victims publicly legible as individuals whose lives were valued and uncovering, if possible, concrete evidence of their time, place, and cause of death. Even more so than nonfictional narratives, fiction seems ideally suited to carrying out such acts of recovery: fiction excels at creating characters whom readers relate to as "possible people," weaving a complete human story from the scant details that remain in the wake of a disappearance and providing a sense of closure to an individual's life story when it is intentionally denied.[2] Because the imaginative work of the fiction writer readily spans geographic distance, moreover, fictional narratives can be created and circulated abroad, beyond the reach of official censorship. But the very conditions of disappearance that make this an urgent project also call into question its putative goal: advocating for victims who cannot speak for themselves. Given that the majority of disappeared people do not survive their initial detention, recovering these victims through narrative is always already a melancholic gesture, since the moment in which that individual's fate could be altered is likely already past. Indeed, continuing to demand the immediate and safe return of victims years or even decades later, as in the well-known case of the Madres de Plaza de Mayo in Argentina, is an effective rhetorical strategy precisely to the extent that it renders time out of joint, demanding an outcome that it is already too late to achieve.[3]

Works of fiction that depict disappearance, like the two I consider in this chapter, the film *Missing* (1982) and Michael Ondaatje's novel *Anil's Ghost*, are by necessity even further removed from the victims whose stories they tell. These works reach their audiences long after the events that inspire them and remain in circulation well beyond those conflicts' conclusions. But perhaps more significantly, they offer fictionalized or purely fictional narrative constructs—characters—to circulate in the place of the missing persons they purport to recover. "Charlie," the idealistic writer and loving husband portrayed by actor John Shea, is not the real person, Charles Horman, who was disappeared by the Chilean government, and the construction of him in *Missing* is clearly a strategic one. In *Anil's Ghost*, Ondaatje does not claim to represent real individuals but nevertheless relies heavily on a range of nonfictional sources, including Amnesty International reports, to create a complex effect of verisimilitude in which the names and identities of actual victims appear alongside characters who are purely narrative constructs. This is not necessarily a bad thing; as I've suggested, fictional characters can capture the imaginations and spark the emotions of readers far more effectively than the scant details about disappeared people provided by nonfictional human rights reports. Nevertheless, our ability to think critically about fictional accounts of disappearance—either literary or, in this case, filmic—requires us to think carefully about the similarities and differences between characters and people, and the ethical implications of substituting one in the place of the other.

Recognizing that these works (and likely many other works of human rights fiction) cannot by their very nature intercede in a timely way to protect the lives of particular victims leaves us to consider: What, then, is the nature of their rhetorical appeal to their readers at a distance? Both *Missing* and *Anil's Ghost* were created at a remove from the violent conflicts they depict. *Missing* was produced in the United States, directed by the noted international filmmaker Costa-Gavras, and released to a U.S. audience almost a decade after the 1973 Chilean coup during which it is set. Ondaatje, a writer of international reputation living in Canada, visited his native Sri Lanka to research *Anil's Ghost*, but wrote, published, and circulated his novel at a remove from that country's protracted civil war; published in 2000, it takes place sometime during the especially violent period "from the mid-1980s to the early 1990s."[4] To the extent that these works prompt their readers to take action to combat human rights abuses, therefore, their advocacy can only serve victims other than the particular individuals they depict (who may themselves be partially or completely imaginative constructs). Speaking to audiences who are distant in both time and space, *Missing* and *Anil's Ghost* instead seek to cultivate an ethos, a shared sense of ethical responsibility that, as John Su has suggested, can be recognized and acted upon only belatedly, in relation to events other than those that initially inspire it.[5] Both these works acknowledge that if they are salvaging something from the scene of disappearance, it is something far less tangible than a person or even a body; rather, their audiences must discover something in the stories of Charlie or "Sailor," the anonymous skeleton Anil identifies, that can be generalized to other victims and other contexts.

Indeed, despite the mimetic realness of the characters and settings that these works construct, and the representational authority that this effect of verisimilitude confers on them, works like *Missing* and *Anil's Ghost* can only be ethically consequential to the extent that their abiding themes and narrative effects can be mobilized beyond the specific individuals and instances they depict. This recognition, in turn, fundamentally reconfigures our sense of the narrative task these works undertake. If the goal of such works is to counteract the silencing and invisibility that disappearance produces, constructing characters as vividly particular people, rich in mimetic detail, is in and of itself a powerful resistance strategy. But however effectively such characters engage the emotions and imaginations of their audiences, these works choose ultimately to subordinate their mimetic dimension to their thematic dimension, enabling them to be put into circulation as ideas—so much so, in fact, that in certain moments the distinguishing features of specific characters threaten to slip away entirely. In a sense, then, these works recover the disappeared as individuals only to lose them again. This compromise, however, is necessary to their ethical projects: if we were moved to care only about Charlie (a fictional rendering of a long deceased person), and not about people like Charlie, the ethical compass of *Missing* would be narrow indeed. While it is easy (perhaps too easy) to throw one's hands up in despair at the inadequacy of such generalizing moves, that is not a choice that either of these works makes. Instead, by inviting their audiences to engage thematically, to privilege the generalizable over the particular, they create messages—and ethical effects—that are potentially portable to other victims and future conflicts.

More troubling than this shift away from mimetic particularity, which transforms particular individuals into representative types, are the blind spots that define these works' privileged thematic frames, which have the effect of placing whole categories of victims beyond their imaginative reach. In telling the story of an American victim of the Chilean coup—one of a few among thousands of Chileans—*Missing* mobilizes the logic of American exceptionalism to make the case that Charlie's disappearance was unjust, first and foremost, because it violated his rights as a U.S. citizen. Thus, although set in Chile, its abiding message is a clear indictment of the U.S. government, whose covert support for the 1973 coup was increasingly acknowledged by the time of the film's release. Indeed, as Costa-Gavras himself makes clear, the generalizable lesson of his film is not about Chileans, but about the ongoing pattern of U.S. entanglements in Latin American politics, fueled by the anxieties of the Cold War.

Written in a later moment, *Anil's Ghost* makes recourse to the supranational discourse of human rights, which by definition supersede the claims of citizenship on which *Missing* relies. But human rights discourse, which derives from the construct of the "human" as a legible philosophical and legal category, is also marked by its own constitutive limits, as many scholars have observed.[6] In the deterritorialized space of the human that Ondaatje's novel constructs, the aesthetic reigns supreme; thus, the novel celebrates truth as an abstract principle and human life as made legible through the universal language of art, and distances itself from the historical and political particularities of the Sri Lankan conflict. In both cases, the thematic frameworks these works mobilize to speak beyond the particular have their own inherent limits, which place certain kinds of victims—Chilean radicals, in *Missing*, or Sri Lankan peasants, in *Anil's Ghost*—beyond the reach of their recuperative efforts. And while the decision to privilege the thematic over the mimetic is a structural imperative of these works, the choice of thematic frame—and its concomitant erasures—is one for which these works' creators and consumers remain accountable.

How Particular People Become "the Disappeared"

Disappearance is unique in the grim repertoire of human rights abuses that, due to a growing culture and discourse of human rights activism, has become increasingly visible in recent decades. Because their detention is not officially acknowledged, the disappeared suffer a fate that is fundamentally different from that of recognized combatants or accused criminals, who are officially captured or arrested and placed on trial. Although their treatment at the hands of the state may also be unjust, these individuals, unlike the disappeared, receive a form of official and public recognition. The term "disappearance," therefore, while evocatively describing the effects of secret, extrajudicial detention, is also potentially misleading: by implying that victims have simply ceased to exist, it effaces the agency of perpetrators and reifies the erasure they attempt to carry out. As Alice Nelson explains, "from the moment of their disappearance, missing people were relegated to a perverse limbo in which the state not only denied their deaths, but also attempted to negate their lives by claiming that the disappeared never existed."[7]

For this reason, human rights groups such as Amnesty International make a point of challenging the discursive erasure of the disappeared: "Amnesty International puts the term [disappearance] in quotation marks to emphasize that the victim has in reality not simply vanished. The victim's whereabouts and fate, concealed from the outside world, are known by someone. Someone decided what would happen to the victim; someone decided to conceal it. Someone is responsible."[8] As Amnesty International makes clear, the language of "disappearance" itself risks capitulating to the logic of its perpetrators, who efface their own responsibility as they deny the very existence of their victims. Indeed, the silencing of the disappeared is often almost total; held in secret prisons, they are rarely able to communicate with the outside world, and most do not survive their detention. Moreover, the systematic regimes of torture that frequently accompany disappearance make it extremely difficult for those who do survive to speak publicly about their experiences.[9]

Disappearance is not only a brutally effective means of silencing individual victims; it also imposes a coerced silence on the broader population. Rather than concealing the fact that people are being disappeared, perpetrators make abductions highly visible as a threat to discipline onlookers and render them complicit.[10] Thus, despite the fact that disappearance is often a matter of common knowledge, the climate of fear it produces prevents it from being acknowledged or condemned, giving rise to an enforced, collective blindness that Diana Taylor has termed "percepticide."[11] Although her subject is Argentina's so-called Dirty War, which differed in important ways from both the Chilean and Sri Lankan conflicts,

Taylor's insights into the representational strategies involved in disappearance are illuminating. As she points out, "the military violence could have been relatively invisible, as the term *disappearance* suggests. The fact that it wasn't indicates that the population as a whole was the intended target, positioned by means of the spectacle. People had to deny what they saw and, by turning away, collude with the violence around them."[12] In a climate like the one Taylor describes, representing the disappeared becomes difficult, if not impossible, in the public sphere. This coerced, public silencing contributes to the spectral quality that victims of disappearance assume: although they exist, their bodies, living or dead, are inaccessible; and although their loss is grieved by their families and community, it cannot be publicly acknowledged.

In the context of such widespread, coerced public blindness, narrating the lives and experiences of the disappeared constitutes an urgent and dangerous form of resistance. As Nelson explains, "Even without a body to serve as physical proof of their existence, . . . missing people did continue to exist through the ways in which other people reconstructed them discursively, by telling stories that bore witness to those individuals' lives within a community."[13] Those within a zone of conflict often go to heroic lengths to represent the disappeared, using methods and media that range from graffiti to unauthorized theater performances to the photographs of their missing children displayed by the Madres de Plaza de Mayo. At the heart of all these strategies is the conviction that the disappeared, though physically absent, can be brought to life through representations that make them legible as victims. Given the risk of producing resistant representations at home, however, narratives of disappearance are often created abroad, intended for an international, rather than domestic, audience. Located beyond the reach of official censorship and coerced silence, authors writing at a distance from a conflict have much more freedom in representing it. And by distributing their narratives broadly, these authors endeavor to make disappearance visible to people who have not directly experienced it and who, free from the fear that controls those in the conflict zone, might be better able to respond and intervene. While recognizing its limitations, James Dawes argues for the importance of such storytelling, which communicates human rights abuses to international audiences: "One of the most important premises of contemporary human rights work is that effective dissemination of information can change the world. . . . Individuals can be inspired to donate time and money; governments, particularly those dependent on foreign aid, can be pressured into altering their behavior."[14]

To the extent that such narratives are effective, in Dawes's terms, they are often strategic, consciously or unconsciously informed by the circuits they will travel. As Kay Schaffer and Sidonie Smith remind us, narratives of human rights abuses are inherently shaped by the contexts of their production, circulation, and reception, and the representations of disappearance in *Missing* and *Anil's Ghost* are no exception. Schaffer and Smith invite us to consider how "modes of circulation impact upon the expectations of the teller, the structure of the story, and the mode of address to different kinds of audiences," as well as the ways in which "contexts of reception direct and contain the ethical call of stories and their appeals for redress."[15] Despite obvious differences in context and medium, I will suggest, both *Missing* and *Anil's Ghost* rely on similar strategies to traverse the distance between their creators, their consumers, and the conflicts they depict. Indeed, although literary and filmic texts are produced and circulated in importantly different ways, both share certain fundamental narrative elements, like character, plot, and progression, that operate similarly to create an effect of verisimilitude that is essential to the work of recovery these works attempt to carry out. In particular, both *Missing* and *Anil's Ghost* rely on the creation of vividly rendered characters whose inner experiences are the medium through which the conflict itself is depicted and interpreted. While factual information about ongoing conflicts or documented human rights abuses is often subject to suppression or distortion, the work of characterization, which requires not fact but believability, can proceed unhindered when information is withheld. By telling character-driven stories, these works claim an authority for themselves that is unique to fiction, shifting the burden of proof away from the forms of factual information that can be suppressed through censorship and coercion, and toward the kinds of fictionalized interiority that novelists and filmmakers are experts at constructing.

The creation of sympathetic, three-dimensional characters is a key mechanism through which both novel and film appeal to audiences who might be unfamiliar with, or actively misinformed about, the conflicts and victims they depict. In particular, both works leverage the properties of progression to introduce readers to the disappeared with the authority of the present tense. In *Missing*, the first portion of the film is devoted to establishing Charlie's fundamental likeability and strength of character, before his disappearance allows his identity and character to be contested. Similarly, a surprise twist at the end of *Anil's Ghost* makes Sarath, one of the novel's central characters, into a victim whose true nature is confirmed, rather than denied, by his disappearance. In both cases, the mimetic dimension of these characters is richly rendered and explicitly counteracts the dominant narratives that would paint the disappeared as anonymous and dispensable: they are particular people, with recognizable traits and meaningful relationships. But, as I will suggest, this is ultimately an effect that neither work is able to maintain. While these works initially set out to bring particular victims to life, the imperative to make their meaning portable ultimately causes them to privilege the thematic at the expense of the mimetic. Thus Charlie, the individual, recedes as the film increasingly strives to reinforce his exemplary status as an idealistic American young man. And Anil's discovery of Sailor's identity ultimately becomes marginal to the novel's central dynamics. These disappearances—the gradual erosion of the individuating details that bring these characters to life as possible people—are in fact an appropriate and necessary response to the untimeliness of much human rights fiction: by subordinating the particular to the general, *Missing* and *Anil's Ghost* ensure that their stories, and any real-world action they might inspire, remain urgent and relevant, even as the conflicts they depict recede into recent history.

Charlie Horman, the Quintessential American

In depicting the events of the Chilean coup, *Missing* faced the challenge of giving a human face to the victims of a regime that received both covert support and overt recognition from the U.S. government.[16] Released in 1982, *Missing* tells the story of Charles Horman, an American expatriate who disappeared during the early days of the 1973 coup, which deposed the democratically elected socialist government of President Salvador Allende and installed a repressive military junta led by General Augusto Pinochet in its place.[17] Despite the fact that the regime's victims were overwhelmingly Chilean citizens, *Missing* focuses almost exclusively on Charlie and, to a lesser extent, the fellow American expatriates who comprise his circle of friends. Beginning during the tense days preceding the coup, the film follows Charlie and his friend Terry (Melanie Mayron) on an ill-fated trip to Viña del

Mar, where they stumble upon damning evidence of the United States' involvement in orchestrating the overthrow of the Allende government—evidence that, the film strongly implies, Charlie is killed in order to suppress.[18] After Charlie's disappearance, his father, Ed (Jack Lemmon), and his wife, Beth (Sissy Spacek), search tirelessly to find him, to receive an official account of why he was detained, and ultimately, to reveal the U.S. government's complicity in his disappearance. At every turn, the Hormans are blocked by Chilean and American government officials, who deny that Charlie was arrested or imply that his bohemian lifestyle and left-leaning politics justified his disappearance. Thus, much of the film is devoted to painting an alternate picture of Charlie that can counteract this official narrative.

The film's first scene, which plays during the opening credits, perfectly illustrates its strategy of placing Charlie—first as an individual, and later as a representative victim—at the center of its narrative project. As the title fades, we see Charlie through the partially open window of a car. He is intently watching a group of children playing soccer, visible to the film's viewers as a distorted reflection in the glass of the car window. Tense, ominous background music contrasts with the innocent scene. Our focus shifts momentarily, first to the smiling face of Terry, who is also watching the game, then briefly to the children themselves, before we witness the arrival of a truck full of heavily armed soldiers. As the soldiers climb down from the truck and the children disperse in fear, we again see the scene as a reflection in the car window, literally projected onto Charlie in the position of the observer. More than just creative cinematography, this inventive shot establishes a perspective emblematic of that which the film as a whole will employ: as viewers, our focus is trained on Charlie, whom we are invited to read through his reaction to the incident unfolding in front of him, and it is in and through our investment in Charlie's story that we witness the coup itself. Like this scene, in which the threat of violence serves primarily as an opportunity to shed light on Charlie's character, the film as a whole functions as an extended debate over Charles Horman's identity and, by extension, his legibility as a victim.

In stark contrast to the anonymous bodies or empty statistics that frequently constitute the only documented evidence of the disappeared, Charlie is highly visible—almost hypervisible—in the film's early scenes. These scenes play a crucial role in establishing him as an empathetic character and an admirable man: we watch him worry about and lovingly comfort his wife, carefully and courageously navigate an encounter with police, and idealistically attempt to intervene on behalf of a stranger seized by security forces. The film's ability to represent Charlie with the authority of the present tense is unique to fiction, since nonfictional representations of the disappeared are, by definition, inevitably retrospective. Disappearance intentionally creates ambiguity and uncertainty; *Missing*, in contrast, places its viewers in the empowering position of knowing the "truth" about Charlie in the face of the competing narratives that will be put forward in the wake of his disappearance. By the time that event occurs, almost thirty minutes into the film, we feel as if we know Charlie personally and, based on that knowledge, can recognize and resist his attempted erasure. In particular, when Ed Horman arrives in Santiago to search for his son, voicing many of the assumptions that mainstream American viewers might have held about a liberal expatriate like Charlie, we are prepared to recognize them as misguided. As viewers of the film, we have already come to understand what Ed initially fails to grasp: that Charlie need not have "done anything wrong" to "get himself arrested."

As much as Ed and Beth's actual search, their ongoing debate about Charlie's identity drives the majority of the film. At the start of the film, Ed, a conservative and devout New York businessman, sees his son as irresponsible and lazy, a dissolute liberal who has carelessly gotten himself in trouble in a foreign country, when he should have stayed at home and "paid . . . attention to the basics." He is disappointed and embarrassed by his son's choice to "be a writer" rather than pursue a professional career and dismayed by what he interprets as Charlie's aversion to hard work. Ed's doubts about his son are echoed by the numerous U.S. government officials depicted in the film, who suggest both implicitly and explicitly that Charlie was a radical and an agitator who deserved his fate. Beth, however, offers a counternarrative of Charlie as an idealist, a childlike dreamer, and a man of principle. Sharing anecdotes, home movies, and Charlie's art and writing with Ed, Beth corroborates the image of Charlie that the film has already firmly established and that Ed himself eventually comes to embrace: a whimsical and generous man with a clear sense of right and wrong and a penchant for note-taking that ultimately lands him in unexpected danger.

Even as the film endeavors to render Charlie as a particular individual, however, Charlie's exceptional status as an American stands out, inviting viewers to recognize him as a specific type of victim within the larger context of the Chilean coup. The choice to focus on an American certainly reflects the film's intended audience and supports its larger narrative and political stakes. Directed by Costa-Gavras, a noted international director recognized for his political films, *Missing* was produced in the context of the mainstream U.S. movie industry: released by Universal Pictures for a U.S. popular audience, it features prominent American actors like Jack Lemmon and Sissy Spacek in starring roles. All of the film's major characters are Americans, and its central ideological debate is not over the justness of the Pinochet regime or its violent rise to power, but rather about the American values of freedom, independence, and democracy, as embodied in culture and enacted in law. Charlie's reassurance to Terry that he is safe because he's an American—which he pronounces "Amurikin," with a comically exaggerated Texas accent—is in essence the argument of the film itself: Charlie is an American, despite his left-leaning sympathies, adventuresome spirit, and youthful naïveté, and should have been protected, rather than victimized, by the long arm of his own government's presence overseas.

Despite making a clear and persuasive case that the U.S. government sanctioned Charles Horman's disappearance, the film concludes with Ed Horman asserting his confidence in the integrity of the U.S. legal system. Boarding a plane back to the States, Ed defiantly announces his intention to sue the American consul, and to the consul's dismissive acknowledgement that, "Well, I guess that's your privilege," he emphatically responds, "No, that's my right!" Ed's unshaken faith in the U.S. legal system stands in stark contrast to the film's depiction of Chile as a place where government officials brazenly tap the Hormans' hotel phones and civilians can be summarily shot for violating curfew. Ed's final statement makes this distinction explicit: "I just thank God that we live in a country where we can still put people like you in jail," he declares to the American officials who failed to protect his son. This logic of American exceptionalism is ultimately the basis on which the film makes its case that Charlie's disappearance, in particular, was unjust.

Thus, like countless other works before and since, *Missing* uses its foreign setting as a foil to establish America's distinctiveness among nations and its attendant rights and responsibilities on the world stage; Chile is its setting, but not the primary object of its concern or critique. Indeed, for Costa-Gavras, who saw events in Chile as representative of U.S. interventions elsewhere in Latin America, the film offers a more expansive commentary on U.S. foreign policy: "Universal [Pictures] would have liked to put at the beginning of the film, 'Chile, September 1973.' By saying that, though, it becomes a local problem, and it also becomes a historical thing—far away, ten years ago, who remembers that? But I think these things are still happening. It could be Argentina, it could be El Salvador. People are disappearing all over the world."[19] As these comments make clear, for Costa-Gavras, the Chilean coup exemplifies the broader phenomenon of political violence in Latin America, a phenomenon inseparable, in the Cold War climate of the 1970s and 1980s, from the U.S. policy of military intervention to prevent the spread of communism. Framed in this way, the story of Charles Horman's disappearance in 1973 dramatizes a much broader principle: that through its interventionist foreign policy, the U.S. continues to fall short of its own ideals in ways that threaten the fundamental rights of its own citizens.

In order for *Missing* to make its case that Charlie's disappearance was unjust, according to this exceptionalist logic, his generic status as an American citizen must trump particular details like his leftist politics or his ill-advised inquisitiveness. Thus, as the film progresses, this thematic function of Charlie's character—his status as an upstanding (and thus implicitly rights-bearing) American citizen—comes to overshadow the mimetic function, his identity as an individual. To do this, the film repeatedly underscores the similarities between Charlie and his father, Ed, drawing on familiar formulas of gender and class to do so. Contrary to Ed's assumptions, Charlie does know the meaning of hard work, putting in eighteen-hour days translating for and editing a small, independent news magazine. And like his father, Charlie is a family man who has "paid ... attention to the basics," making a life and a home for himself and his wife in Santiago that Beth remembers as "one of the happiest homes I've ever had." Although he may not share Ed's faith in "God, country, and Wall Street," Charlie is just as courageous and idealistic as his father: when Ed impulsively attempts to intervene in and stop a violent incident, we are reminded that just weeks earlier, his son did "the same damn dumb thing." By revealing the ways in which Charlie embodies the masculine norms of hard work, responsibility, and courage that his father also values, the film emphasizes the filial bond between them and reaffirms Charlie's status as, like Ed, a citizen and a patriot.

Emphasizing Charlie's status as a representative American in such normative terms, however, necessarily excludes both American radicals and all Chileans from the compass of the film's recuperative effort. The implicit distinction between good American citizens and leftist political agitators is reinforced by the film's treatment of another disappeared expatriate, Frank Teruggi (Joe Regalbuto). Like many others in the film, the Teruggi character is loosely based on a real person of the same name; in the film, Teruggi represents the committed leftist, a staunch supporter of Chile's socialist experiment, whose zeal contrasts with the innocent enthusiasm of a "political neophyte" like Charlie. Teruggi's disappearance is one of the other "cases" that the consulate is pursuing, but the film suggests that the American officials are even less concerned with his fate than they are with Charlie's. Indeed, these officials' own statements unintentionally reveal their tacit belief that leftist "radicals" like Teruggi are not the kind of Americans entitled to the intervention and protection of the consulate. Sketching an outlandish scenario in which Charlie staged his own kidnapping, they suggest he might have done so to tarnish the reputation of the regime by "mak[ing] it look like they're arresting

Americans." Beth is quick to point out their oversight: "They *are* arresting Americans, or don't David Holloway and Frank Teruggi count!" Certainly, the film intends to suggest that Americans like Teruggi do count, but by emphasizing Charlie's political disengagement and naïveté, the film itself reproduces the logic it attributes to the consul, which excludes so-called radicals from the category of true citizens.

Even more than American radicals, the thousands of Chileans murdered by the Pinochet regime are necessarily marginalized by the film's emphasis on the rights of American citizens. There are notably few Chilean characters in *Missing*, and even fewer civilians. The one Chilean leftist to whom we are introduced, initially counted among the missing, is eventually revealed to have been in hiding and returns safely to his family—in reality a highly unlikely scenario. The scenes in which Ed and Beth search for Charlie in Santiago's overflowing hospitals, morgues, and detention centers represent the film's most sustained engagement with the widespread violence that followed in the wake of the coup, and the visual disproportion of these scenes, which reduce Chilean victims to the status of scenery, reveals the limits of its larger thematic frame: although these people, too, have been disappeared, they are the citizens of a foreign government, whom the United States has no particular obligation to protect. The erasure of these victims, who never rise to the status of characters, is a direct consequence of the exceptionalist logic on which *Missing* relies to frame its broader political critique.

This selective vision does not, however, go entirely unacknowledged in the film. In a pivotal scene, Ed and Beth finally get permission to search for Charlie in the National Stadium, an improvised prison camp where the military regime detained, tortured, and murdered hundreds and perhaps thousands of people in the early days of the coup. When Ed and Beth emerge onto the playing field, the image revealed to viewers is shocking: as the camera pans across the stands, we see that they are full of people, all prisoners, whose ragged appearance and improvised shelters suggest that they have been in captivity for some time. Over the loudspeaker, Ed and Beth identify themselves and address Charlie by name, searching for him in vain among the crowds in the stands. The privileged status that Ed and Beth enjoy is emphasized by the Chilean colonel's introduction of them, which is one of the few instances of subtitled dialogue in the film: "We're going to permit this American who is looking for his son to speak here. Keep quiet [and pay attention]."[20] As this introduction makes clear, Ed Horman's ability to search for his son in the stadium is entirely contingent on both men's status as U.S. citizens, a fact that is not lost on at least one of the prisoners. In response to Ed's appeal, a young man who appears to be about Charlie's age, with a similar hairstyle, rushes forward, and Ed initially mistakes this prisoner for his son. The visual effect of this moment is unsettling, even after viewers realize the mistake that Ed has made (and perhaps they themselves have made as well). Leaning on the chain link fence that separates the stands from the field, the prisoner sarcastically addresses the Hormans in accented English. "My father cannot come here. But how about some ice cream with my dinner, *Coronel* Espinoza?"

This scene, in which an individual Chilean victim is able to be rendered visible only by being mistaken for Charlie, highlights not only the slipperiness of Charlie's identity, which the film has gone to significant lengths to establish, but also, more troublingly, the selective vision that allows one American to overshadow the many Chileans with parents similarly desperate for knowledge of their fates. And ironically, by usurping the discursive space reserved for Charlie in order to make his own impossible demands, the irreverent prisoner once again becomes invisible, for the optic of the film reduces him to Charlie's uncanny double. Moreover, by this point in the film, viewers realize that this man's attempt to make himself visible will likely cost him his life.

The prisoner's outburst in the stadium is hardly necessary to the film's plot; indeed, as the Chilean writer Ariel Dorfman has pointed out, "the scene is touching but implausible" given the disciplinary power of the detention center.[21] Its inclusion challenges us to ask, as Dorfman does, "What about him? What about the son whose father could not go to the stadium to search for him?"[22] By making Charlie's identity as an upstanding American citizen central to its project of recovery, *Missing* may succeed in making him legible as a victim and transforming his story into a more wide-ranging critique of the U.S. government's pattern of un-American actions on the world stage. But as a consequence, Chileans like the irreverent prisoner cannot be brought to life as characters with either individuating features or larger messages conveyed in and through their lives and deaths.

"The Ascendancy of the Idea" in *Anil's Ghost*

Anil's Ghost, like *Missing*, revolves around efforts to identify a single, individual victim of the larger conflict it depicts. Set during one of the most intensely violent periods in Sri Lanka's civil war, which pitted the country's majority Sinhala government against both Tamil separatists in the north and armed militants in the south, the novel initially presents its readers with a mystery: Anil, a forensic pathologist representing an international human rights organization, and Sarath, the government archaeologist with whom she is paired, discover a contemporary skeleton in an ancient burial site.[23] Knowing that the skeleton's location in a controlled archaeological site strongly implicates the government, they undertake to identify the victim, whom they nickname "Sailor," and to document his disappearance. As the novel progresses, however, its focus shifts from Anil's effort to identify Sailor through forensic science to the lives of the other Sri Lankan characters, each of whom has found a way to cope with the conflict that rages around them. By the end of the novel, Anil's search for truth in "bones and sediment" has receded to the background, and the novel's shifting temporality and roving, omniscient narration instead present readers with a collage of what Sarath describes as "character and nuance and mood" (259).

Anil, enamored of both the methods of forensic science and its underlying empiricism, initially occupies the center of the novel, which traces her efforts to discover the identity of the skeleton she has found. To identify an anonymous victim like Sailor, Anil seeks to uncover "the permanent truths" evidenced by his remains (64). Eventually, she successfully identifies Sailor based on the "markers of occupation" on his bones, which reveal his past labor as a toddy tapper and a miner, which in turn allows her to discover his village, his name—Ruwan Kumara—and the circumstances of his disappearance (177). Even as Anil and Sarath move closer to identifying Sailor's remains, however, the novel's focus shifts away from the evidence-based process of forensic analysis and toward the inner lives of a diverse cast of characters that Ondaatje has introduced in the preceding pages: Sarath and his brother Gamini, a physician; Palipana, the aging scholar; and Ananda, a local artisan whom Anil and Sarath hire to create a facial reconstruction of Sailor. Amid the chaos of war, these characters distance themselves from the facts of the violence that surrounds them, instead seeking truth and transcendence in the realm of the aesthetic.

If *Anil's Ghost* offers two models of recovering the identity and humanity of the disappeared—the empirical methods of Anil and the aestheticism of the novel's other characters—it is clear by the end of the novel which model it privileges. Outside the context of the Sri Lankan conflict, Anil's focus on the details of forensic science in popular movies (where exactly is Lee Marvin's character shot in the opening of *Point Blank*?) reveals a myopic ignorance of the films' broader narrative and imaginative stakes. Within the conflict zone, this empiricism not only prevents her from seeing the bigger picture, but also, in doing so, exposes her and those around her to danger. Despite establishing the "details of [Sailor's] age and posture" and eventually allowing her to match those details with a name and a rudimentary biography, Anil's forensic work tells her "nothing about the world Sailor had come from" (176), and in the context of official repression, the evidence in which she places so much faith is vulnerable to suppression or distortion. Ultimately, when the government confiscates both Sailor's skeleton and her research notes, Anil is left without recourse, and Sarath must sacrifice his life to allow her to escape the country with enough evidence to document Sailor's murder.

In contrast, the character of Palipana, Sarath's disgraced and reclusive mentor, epitomizes the nonliteral interpretive practices that the novel advocates. Palipana was trained as an archaeologist, but his preferred description of himself as an "epigraphist" suggests a more oblique, less literal relationship between the ancient writings he studies and the meaning he finds in them (78). Although Palipana's subject is the ancient past, the novel clearly links the "political tides and royal eddies of the island in the sixth century" to the political violence in present-day Sri Lanka (81). As Palipana's own eyesight fades, the "illegal story" he finds recorded in interlinear inscriptions is "how one hid or wrote the truth when it was necessary to lie" (105). Ondaatje suggests that despite Palipana's disgrace within the academic community, which rejects his findings as fabricated, his practice of reading and definition of truth are the right ones for the times. His traumatized, orphaned niece, who rightly distrusts the pretense of safety at the government orphanage where she is initially taken, comes into her own under Palipana's care and tutelage. Like the shifting, elusive truth that Palipana seeks, the phrase she chisels into the rock at the edge of a lake to commemorate him after his death "appears and disappears" with the light and the level of the water (107). An almost sacred figure in the novel, Palipana is emblematic of the imaginative, aesthetic work of recovering the truth of a life from the silence of official history.

Ananda also responds to disappearance through creative acts of representation rather than factual reconstruction. Ananda's wife, Sirissa, is, like Sailor, a victim of the war, and her disappearance prompts him to abandon his work as a ceremonial painter of Buddhist statues and take up grueling and dangerous work in the gem mines. When Anil and Sarath hire him to reconstruct a likeness of Sailor's head, the project becomes a way of challenging the uncertainty and erasure that disappearance produces: Ananda literally puts flesh on Sailor's bones, creating a recognizable face from an unrecognizable skull. Like other fictional representations of the disappeared, and like the novel itself, Ananda's reconstruction dispels the uncertainty of sparse facts to render an unknown victim as "a specific person"; indeed it is the unmistakable individuality of the face he sculpts that first strikes Anil, to whom it seems to reveal "not just how someone possibly looked," but rather "a distinct personality" (184). The face Ananda creates, however, is not strictly speaking a likeness of Sailor, but rather a representation of "what he wants of the dead," displaying "a calm Ananda had known in his wife, [and] a peacefulness he wanted for any victim" (184, 187). Like the characters that populate Ondaatje's novel, the face Ananda sculpts has all the distinctiveness of an individual yet corresponds to no person in particular. Through his sculpture, Ananda recovers the disappeared on an imaginative rather than factual level, bringing them to life not as accurate reconstructions, but rather as persuasively particular possible people who can inspire powerful emotions in those, like Anil and Sarath, who regard them.

In a similar way, Ondaatje's novel is ultimately less invested in the facts that Anil uncovers than in the insights her search occasions into the novel's central characters; as Manav Ratti has suggested, this focus on character is an aesthetic strategy that "challenges the limits of the law's abstract univocality" and provides an alternative to the reductive framework that Anil's methods offer.[24] Indeed, although Anil's quest to identify Sailor initially gives the novel the shape of a mystery or thriller, the novel soon diverges from such a linear, plot-driven structure.[25] Its narration is elliptical and nonsequential, frustrating any teleological drive toward the truth, and the abiding sense of futility surrounding the political and legal processes in Sri Lanka (Anil herself acknowledges that "in all the token police investigations, not one murder charge had been made during the troubles," 176) signals readers not to hold out much hope that identifying Sailor's remains will lead to a satisfying conclusion in which perpetrators are held to account. What drives the novel, as in *Missing*, are not the facts of the case, but rather the richly detailed personal stories of its characters, who struggle to understand and trust one another. Anil, a former champion swimmer, has not been back to Sri Lanka since her parents died in a car crash. Having escaped a bad marriage to a fellow Sri Lankan émigré, and ended her relationship with a married lover by stabbing him in the arm with a pocket knife, she is currently exchanging postcards with her girlfriend, a fellow forensic scientist in Arizona, who is suffering from Alzheimer's disease. Sarath is the older of two sons, who is passionate about the work of archaeology and has scrupulously kept his distance from all sides of the ongoing civil war. His brother, Gamini, is an emergency services doctor who has become addicted to amphetamines; in love with the woman who will become Sarath's wife, Gamini is there to treat her in the hospital, and witness her final moments, when she later commits suicide. More than the fragmentary evidence that Anil and Sarath uncover, the complex biographies and rich inner lives of these characters drive the novel, and the quest to uncover information about the living, rather than the dead, ultimately motivates its progression.

If *Anil's Ghost* suggests that the imaginative work of characterization, rather than the scientific work of documentation, is the best and only way to recover the disappeared, the unexpected final turn in which Sarath himself becomes a victim of disappearance represents the culmination of that logic. Although Anil is able to glean a significant number of biographical facts about Ruwan Kumara, those facts are never enough to bring him to life in the imaginations of the novel's readers, for whom he remains, at best, a generic portrait of a Sri Lankan peasant. Sarath, by contrast, is a complex, three-dimensional character whom readers have been deeply engaged with over the course of several hundred pages. Again, as in *Missing*, the novel does not need to work backward from remains to tell Sarath's story; instead, we've come to know Sarath intimately before he is transformed, through disappearance, into an anonymous victim.

As a result, Sarath's disappearance corroborates, rather than conceals, the true nature of his character: by sacrificing his life to protect Anil and her findings, Sarath finally proves to Anil, and the novel's readers, where his loyalties lie. And when Gamini sees his brother's body in the morgue, the marks on Sarath's body tell a profoundly personal story. His familiar scars evoke memories of childhood mishaps, as Gamini recalls, "The gash of scar on the side of your elbow you got crashing a bike on the Kandy hill. This scar I gave you hitting you with a cricket stump" (287). Even the tactics of Sarath's torturers, inferred from his injuries, corroborate rather than conceal his essential nature: "It was the face they went for in some cases," Gamini reflects. "They could in their hideous skill sniff out vanity. But they had not touched Sarath's face" (289–90). This literary rendering of disappearance is able to provide certainty, rather than uncertainty, precisely because of the mechanisms of fictional storytelling, which give us privileged prior access to the interiority of a particular victim and contrive for him to be conveniently discovered by a family member with both personal insight and medical expertise.

Like *Missing*, therefore, *Anil's Ghost* chooses to foreground the stories of three-dimensional characters, rather than the larger political context that provides the occasion for telling them, a strategy that reflects and responds to the conditions of the novel's production, circulation, and reception. An expatriate educated in England and residing, teaching, and writing in Canada, and a past winner of the Booker Prize, Ondaatje writes for an international literary audience who may have little knowledge or concern for the particularities of the Sri Lankan conflict. By privileging the inner lives of its characters over the vicissitudes of the conflict that surrounds them, *Anil's Ghost* delivers an engaging narrative that is geared toward the interests and competencies of such readers. Not surprisingly, therefore, the novel has been criticized for providing a depoliticized depiction of the Sri Lankan civil war. In his review for *The Nation*, Tom LeClair accuses Ondaatje of "turn[ing] away from politics to personal lives," and Qadri Ismail dismisses the novel as "not much more than the typically flippant gesture towards Sri Lanka often produced by the West."[26] Indeed, by focusing on the senseless loss of life, rather than the underlying social and political causes of the Sri Lankan conflict, *Anil's Ghost* exemplifies a broader phenomenon that Ismail elsewhere identifies: the emergence in the post–Cold War era of "violence" as an analytical category.

As Ismail argues, the "violence" attributed to the Sri Lankan civil war is distinguished by its fundamental incomprehensibility, or what he calls, with intentional echoes of Conrad, its "horror."[27] Unlike other historical conflicts, which could be made legible through the political frameworks of "U.S. imperialism, communist adventurism, national liberation, [or] Marxist revolution," the contemporary eruption of violence in Sri Lanka, like that in Bosnia and Rwanda, cannot be assimilated into narratives of the nation's political modernity. Unable to provide a political explanation for acts of seemingly inhuman cruelty and destruction taking place in "strange non-Western places," Westerners define them as "violence," an irreducible cultural phenomenon that is not subjected to further analysis.[28] Significantly, as Ismail points out, the production of violence as "a global phenomenon" allows for a logic of analogy, which makes sense of the Sri Lankan conflict "not by attending to its concerns, its debates, its singularity," but rather "by comparing it to other violent, horrible, and incomprehensible places."[29] It is precisely this logic of analogy, then, that *Anil's Ghost* employs to reach beyond the particularities of Sri Lanka in the 1980s, providing an account of senseless loss and aesthetic transcendence that resonates more broadly with its cosmopolitan readership.

The treatment of Anil's forensic work in Ondaatje's novel clearly reflects this understanding of violence as a global phenomenon that is symptomatic of a broader postnational reality. The novel's first scene depicts Anil at work excavating a mass grave in Guatemala, where she and her team are respectfully looked after by the grief-stricken family members of the victims, and elsewhere the novel refers to her work in the Congo. For a time, Anil works at forensic laboratories in Oklahoma and Arizona with the remains of the missing and the murdered; though not the victims of political unrest, these individuals too met violent ends, the truth of which can be uncovered by forensic analysis. Anil's skills, the novel suggests, are universal and portable, applicable anywhere there are victims of violence, and their explanatory power, like the acts of violence that require them, are universal and unchanging, "same for Colombo as for Troy" (64). The aesthetic truths that Palipana, Sarath, and Ananda embrace are similarly valued for their universality and, compared to Anil's forensics, are far less subject to censorship or suppression. In one striking example, Sarath recalls how, in the midst of the conflict, he and Palipana were awed to discover ancient carvings on the wall of a cave. In this scene, "the affection or grief" depicted in the carved image of a mother and her child holds as much ethical force for Sarath as information about the disappearances happening around him; both are forms of truth for which he would be willing to give his life, "if the truth were of any use" (157). Like Anil's forensics, Sarath's aesthetic appreciation generalizes violence, equating the grief of this mother from another century with that of contemporary survivors—and, implicitly, suggesting that both are beyond his reach to comprehend or prevent.

If, as Ismail suggests, the notion of "violence" renders all seemingly incomprehensible Third World conflicts equivalent, the novel suggests that "beauty" is the one principle that can survive and ultimately redeem such tragedies, at least to some small but important degree. This thematic frame, which allows the novel's message to resonate beyond its particular setting, however, ultimately compromises the mimetic particularity of its characters, many of whom seem, at certain moments, to share an uncharacteristic love of literature and art most strongly associated with the novel's implied author. In a particularly striking scene, Anil turns to classic works of European fiction, *The Man in the Iron Mask* and *Les Misérables*, to make sense of her experiences of the war. Incongruously for someone whose search for truth is guided by phrases like "the bone of choice would be the femur" (140), Anil praises one of these novels as "so thick with human nature she wished it to accompany her into the afterlife" (54); although her sudden and unexplained love of literature serves the novel's larger thematic needs, it challenges the mimetic illusion of her as an individual with consistent and recognizable traits. Similarly, Gamini and the other doctors in the remote field hospital where he completes his training adopt "a habit . . . of critical marginalia," commenting sarcastically on anything "not clinically or psychologically valid" in the novels they share (230), and Sarath, we're told, can "read a bucket of soil as if it were a complex historical novel" (151), though neither brother has previously expressed any particular literary affinities.

Not only do central characters like Anil and Gamini prove surprisingly protean, but as the novel progresses, and more characters are introduced, the search for universal truths embodied in their experiences gives rise to a logic of archetype that transforms particularizing details into broader thematic tropes. *Anil's Ghost* is filled with doubles who blend into one another: two doctors kidnapped and held captive by insurgents; two local men, Ananda and Gunesena, whom Anil and Sarath employ, either before or after saving their lives. Ananda shares identifying features not only with Gunesena, but also with Ruwan Kumara; it's Ananda's distinctive squatting posture, a habit acquired from working in the gem mines, that allows Anil to recognize that Ruwan Kumara, too, worked in the mines. Gamini and Sarath are a pair of brothers who love and lose the same woman, and the quiet, capable nurse that Gamini admires after the death of Sarath's wife not only is the second married woman with suicidal tendencies to whom he is attracted, but also blends into a veritable cast of quiet, capable nurses who inhabit the novel's various hospitals and laboratories. This effect of doubling, utterly at odds with the individuating logic of identification, contributes to a larger sense that it is not these particular people with whom the novel is most centrally concerned, but rather what they represent: the various ways in which human beings attempt to make sense of, and ultimately transcend, senseless violence and tragedy.[30]

This is a strategy that not only compromises the legibility of individual characters, but also determines which types of people can be brought to life as characters in accordance with the novel's larger thematic aims. Thus, someone like Ruwan Kumara, who does not share the cosmopolitan aesthetic sensibilities that the novel most values, necessarily recedes into the background. Neither Anil's forensic analysis nor Ananda's facial reconstruction are sufficient to render Ruwan Kumara as a particular individual, and the novel's omniscient narrator never ventures into his consciousness. It is "Sailor," the archetypal victim, rather than Ruwan Kumara, toddy tapper and mine worker, in whom the novel is invested; evidence taken from Sailor's remains is what Anil carries with her when she leaves the country to appeal to international authorities, and it is for the principle of truth that Sailor represents, rather than the man, already deceased, that Sarath gives his life. Sarath's own disappearance, in turn, further marginalizes Ruwan Kumara, and the novel is able to represent Sarath's death in the privileged, putatively universal language of Western art in a way that would not have been possible for Ruwan Kumara within the novel's dominant frame. Describing the scene where Gamini finds Sarath's body as "a pietà between brothers," Ondaatje links Gamini's grief to this archetypal image, as well as to the ancient carving that so moved Sarath while he was alive (288). Like the truth conveyed in that carving, the novel suggests, the aesthetic or emotional truth of this moment is the manifestation of an abstract principle, not an actionable call for intervention or redress.

This universalizing strategy, which packages the products of Sri Lanka for export, is not without its costs, as the novel itself makes clear. At one point, Palipana guides a group of archaeology students through a looted cave temple, where bodhisattva statues had been cut away from the walls into which they were carved and sold to Western museums. Palipana's mournful conviction that only "the ascendancy of the idea" survives the ravages of history is belied by the enduring loss of the missing statues, which persist as wounds in the cave walls (12). The fact that the statues were coveted by Western museums attests to the universality of their value and appeal as works of art, and "the ascendancy of the idea" could easily have been used as a justification for their theft in this colonial context. But as the scene makes clear, the statues themselves, as well as the cave site, are profoundly and irrevocably diminished by their removal. Not only were pieces of the works destroyed ("a head lost forever in a river south of the Sind desert," 12), but a dimension of their meaning was lost when they were removed from their original context, as well.

Arguably, the many documentary references that Ondaatje excerpts throughout the novel suffer a similar fate. The names of the disappeared that Ondaatje lists, for example, may be drawn from an actual human rights report but "cannot have the urgency of an Amnesty action appeal in the enduring medium of a cloth-bound novel."[31] As Sophia McClennen and Joseph Slaughter correctly point out, this text within the novel exists uncertainly between the realms of advocacy and art; while something may be gained from its appropriation in Ondaatje's novel, something is surely lost as well.[32] Indeed, the same can be said of the novel as a whole, as an artistic rendering of a past moment in a real-world conflict. What is lost, when *Anil's Ghost* transforms real victims into imaginary characters whose lives and deaths advance a larger theme about the transcendent power of art, I want to suggest, is not only the mimetic particularity of individual victims but, more distressingly, the particular kinds of victims who are least compatible with that theme—of whom Ruwan Kumara is exemplary. Ondaatje's choice to replace nonfictional victims with fictional characters at the center of his novel responds, ethically, to the belatedness of his work relative to the victims whose names appear within it. But the novel's privileged thematic frame, which contributes to its distinctiveness and significance as a work of art, is one that inevitably pushes certain kinds of victims and certain kinds of stories to the margins. To be clear: it's not that it is impossible for a writer like Ondaatje to render such characters in a rich and believable way, or for Western readers of literary fiction to imagine them as three-dimensional individuals. Ondaatje could have written a novel with Ruwan Kumara at its center; it could not, however, have been *this* novel. It is for this choice—not the choice to fictionalize, but the choice of how to fictionalize—that *Anil's Ghost* can and should be held accountable.

The Uncanny Afterlives of Untimely Fictions

As fictional representations of disappearance, both *Missing* and *Anil's Ghost* are flawed, but not, as I have argued, for the reason we might initially think. As works of fiction, these texts do not—and cannot—make direct and timely interventions in the events they depict; instead, they operate indirectly and belatedly, offering their audiences vividly rendered characters and stories with broadly applicable themes that might potentially change the way those audiences think, feel, or act toward other conflicts and other victims at some point in the present or the future. This, in and of itself, is not a betrayal of their aims; it is, instead, an appropriate response to the ethical imperatives of their production, circulation, and reception. Faced with matters of life-or-death importance, *Missing* and *Anil's Ghost* make an effort to tell stories that matter, offering constructs in place of people, and rendering imagined worlds that are necessarily nonconcomitant with the realities they might seem to substitute for. As a part of this process, the logic of recovery, with its emphasis on the individual, is ultimately subordinated to the logic of representativeness, which allows the stories they tell to be mobilized beyond the particular. It is not the fact that these works generalize, but rather the way in which they do so, that leads to their most troubling oversights and omissions, which privilege certain kinds of individuals and victims over others in ways that reinforce familiar differentials of power.

Acknowledging that these texts, despite their seeming urgency, offer at best a belated response to the events that occasioned them also means attending to their afterlives, as they take on new meanings in relation to events their creators could not have anticipated. *Missing*, for instance, has acquired an uncanny resonance since the September 11, 2001, terrorist attacks in the United States. As I have suggested, the logic of American exceptionalism in the film, which underwrites its critique of U.S. foreign policy in Latin America, also denies the possibility that the United States, like Chile, could be a place where rights are violated and injustices are perpetrated in the name of national security. Yet the subsequent practice of referring to the coup, which took place on September 11, 1973, as "Chile's 9/11" allows that chapter of Chilean history to cast a long shadow over recent U.S. policy in defense of the "homeland," including so-called aggressive interrogation techniques and the systematic practice of extraordinary rendition. From a twenty-first-century vantage point, then, the film's critique cuts deeper than initially intended, allowing the events in Chile, one of Latin America's proudest and longest-standing democracies at the time of the coup, to provide its contemporary American viewers with a cautionary tale. This retrospective reading of the film is still one that places America, rather than Chile, at its conceptual center, and it does not negate the film's marginalization of Chilean victims; nevertheless it offers an opportunity for critical reflection that is worth taking seriously.

In a different way, *Anil's Ghost* can be seen to anticipate the critique of human rights discourse that has become more expansive and full-throated in the decades since its publication.[33] In interesting ways, despite its flaws, the novel undercuts the imperialist logic that, as Elizabeth Anker suggests, is a hallmark of what she terms the "human rights bestseller."[34] The trope of the Western hero who brings salvation in the form of human rights ideology and advocacy to the benighted Third World is one that *Anil's Ghost* identifies and self-consciously resists through its conclusion. Although Anil, the cosmopolitan human rights worker, offers the novel's readers a way into Sri Lanka, she does not offer them a way out: her return to the West, fleeing government reprisal, is never narrated. Instead, after Anil discovers that Sarath has orchestrated her escape, the following chapter takes us not forward, to witness her departure, but backward, to a remembered conversation between Gamini and Sarath. As both brothers affirm their commitment to

remain in Sri Lanka, Gamini derisively sketches the typical conclusion of a work of human rights fiction: "American movies, English
books—remember how they all end? . . . The American or the
Englishman gets on a plane and leaves. That's it. The camera leaves
with him" (285). In contrast to this model, *Anil's Ghost* concludes
with Gamini's discovery of Sarath's body, and Ananda's return to
work as a ceremonial painter of Buddhist statues. Ananda recalls
the dead—Sarath, as well as his wife Sirissa—as he carries out his
work; as the narrator explains in this final chapter, "he and the
woman Anil would always carry the ghost of Sarath Diyasena"
(305). The addition of the modifier "the woman" to Anil's name
underscores her ultimate insignificance: from a specific person at
the center of Ondaatje's tale, she has now become someone whose
name, without additional information, might not be sufficient to
summon her to mind. By marginalizing Anil, and the putative uni-
versalism of the human rights discourse associated with her, the
novel avoids, at least to some degree, the Eurocentric tropes that
Gamini parodies.

Recognizing and valuing the ways that works of human rights
fiction like *Missing* and *Anil's Ghost* become ethically consequential as fictional representations of real-world atrocities requires us
to acknowledge the all-important difference between fiction and
reality, but it does not require us to overlook these works' most
unsettling shortcomings. As representations of the disappeared,
both *Missing* and *Anil's Ghost* are marked by enduring silences:
the categories of people whose stories cannot be accommodated
to these works' larger themes and meanings—about the principles
of American democracy, or the transcendent power of art. Rather
than attending only to the complete, compelling narratives of disappearance these texts purport to provide, we should also attend
to their silences, which reveal the shaping effect of their audiences

on the fictions they construct. For members of the international audiences these texts address—American moviegoers and readers of Anglophone literary fiction—to do so is potentially to acknowledge some measure of complicity in these works' representational choices, and their consequent erasures.

4

Haunting Futures and the Dystopian Imagination

Neither Ayi Kwei Armah's 1968 novel, *The Beautyful Ones Are Not Yet Born*, a depiction of life in newly independent Ghana, nor Don DeLillo's *Falling Man*, set in post-9/11 New York City and published in 2007, offers a particularly appealing vision of the social world occupied by its author. In Armah's Ghana, the social life of the nation is dominated by an ethos of unchecked consumption, financed by graft and corruption, that prevents the emergence of a more hopeful and productive vision for the nation's future. In DeLillo's novel, the terrorist attacks of 9/11 signal the end of America's role as an economic and cultural superpower, but in doing so reveal the emptiness and meaninglessness of the late capitalist society whose decline they inaugurate. In both works, characters' past belief in narratives of progress makes their present disillusionment all the more acute; they are haunted in the present by the possible futures they were once, but are no longer, able to imagine. Not surprisingly, these novels' grim visions of the present and the future drew strong negative reactions from many of their initial readers. Reading these works through the lens of dystopian fiction, however, with an eye to their strategies of defamiliarization and structural open-endedness, reveals the way their bleak views of the present can function as a form of future-oriented social critique.

In this chapter I consider how the logic of haunting allows writers like Armah and DeLillo to imagine a different and better future without denying the material and discursive limitations of the present. Writing during historical moments in which imagining otherwise seems both urgently necessary and impossibly compromised, both authors resist simplistic forms of optimism, refusing to take up the flawed rhetorics of change and transformation that are available to them. Instead, through the conventions of dystopian form, these works' intensely negative renderings of contemporary life work to expose the flaws of familiar social and political realities and provide their readers with necessary critical distance. By leaving their representations of societies in crisis open to reinterpretation and rereading, however, *Beautyful Ones* and *Falling Man* remain committed to carrying out clear-eyed social critique while also allowing for the possibility that the future might hold the promise of meaningful change. These works stage encounters with as-yet-unrealized futures that, as in the case of other haunting encounters, are both tantalizingly close and unfathomably different. In doing so, they respond to the ethical imperative to imagine a genuinely different future without forgetting the lessons of the past—in this case, that the language of hope and change itself has proven to be fundamentally compromised and susceptible to abuse. Ultimately, these texts—and our readings of them—are haunted by futures that they themselves cannot presage; as readers, we are invited to step into the ghostly reading positions they map out, and to question whether we can generate the kinds of genuinely different vision they call for.

This chapter breaks the pattern of previous comparisons by considering a work by a white, Western, American author—Don DeLillo—alongside Armah's depiction of his own newly postcolonial nation. Having thus far examined works that explicitly address themselves, at least in part, to majoritarian audiences across boundaries of ethnic, cultural, or national difference, I am intentionally making a somewhat different type of comparison here. *Falling Man* does not speak from the margins; instead, it is a majoritarian work that arrives to us already engaged in the work of decentering itself. The post-9/11 America that DeLillo depicts is quite pointedly not that which many Americans thought they knew prior to the terrorists attacks, nor the idealized construct they rushed to celebrate or defend in the immediate aftermath of those attacks. It is, rather, an America that is, in the novel's own words, "losing the center" it once believed itself to possess.[1] What DeLillo and Armah have in common, therefore, despite their different positioning, is an investment in defamiliarization: a rendering of the here and now that invites readers who recognize themselves in either work to encounter themselves as other. In this sense, the comparison between them is a cross-cultural encounter that I myself am staging, between two works that are primarily addressed to proximate rather than distant audiences. In the same way that the ethical encounter with the other begins with a recognition of difference, these works confront readers with their own ghostly doubles, challenging them to see themselves anew.

Like the accounts of disappearance examined in chapter 3, both *Beautyful Ones* and *Falling Man* are works of fiction with uncanny afterlives, existing as enduring records of the particular historical moments that inspired them. Though many of the conditions described in these works—corruption and economic stratification, hollow consumerism and jingoistic nationalism—persist today, these novels are the product of the past, and we read them now, necessarily, in retrospect. To some degree, hindsight blunts the impact of their extreme pessimism, as subsequent events (persistent neocolonialism and a never-ending war on terror) seem to justify the bleak outlooks that so shocked their initial readers. Reading from the position of the future, however, we are able to put these works' formal politics to the test: Is it possible, from our present vantage point, to imagine the kinds of genuinely different social realities these works call for, but cannot themselves envision? Ultimately, while their pessimism may no longer seem unwarranted, their circular structure resists being transformed into a static image of the past, and their restless impulse toward futurity remains productively unsettling.

The Unpleasant Present

Armah's representation of postindependence Ghana in *The Beautyful Ones Are Not Yet Born* is unrelentingly bleak. The novel's protagonist, referred to throughout simply as "the man," has abandoned the intellectual ambitions of his youth and resigned himself to a job at the Railroad Administration, which he finds thankless and stultifyingly dull. While barely able to support his family on his government paycheck, he is surrounded by flagrant and unabashed corruption, which he rejects on principle despite his desire to provide a better life for his wife and children. The man's refusal to participate in dishonest dealings isolates him from Ghanaian society at large, which he perceives as having enthusiastically embraced corruption in pursuit of "the gleam" of modern amenities and European imports.[2] Although the man rejects the dishonest practices required to attain the gleam, he grudgingly acknowledges its appeal, especially in contrast to the poverty that is its alternative: the novel begins during "Passion Week," the week before payday, when the man and all those around him have barely enough money for food and bus fare (1). "How much hard work," the man skeptically wonders, "before a month's pay would last till the end of the month?" (95).

In a world where corruption is the only route to success, others see the man's honesty not as integrity but as foolishness or cowardice. His wife, Oyo, is particularly dismayed by the man's refusal to participate in what he describes as "the national game," and she ridicules him for lacking the courage to provide her with the lifestyle she desires (55). As Oyo explains, "Everybody is swimming towards what he wants. Who wants to remain on the beach asking the wind 'How...How...How?'" (44). The example of Joe Koomson, the man's former classmate, deepens Oyo's disappointment in her husband. Now a government minister, Koomson is living the life of the "gleam," enjoying privileges formerly reserved for the class of colonial exploiters. His life is filled with luxuries that can only be obtained through corruption and public theft: a chauffeured car; a spacious house in the exclusive, largely white Upper Residential Area; and imported goods like liquor, perfume, a German radio set, a wig for his wife, and beautiful clothes and toys for his children. Although Oyo knows that the Koomsons' lifestyle is financed by dishonesty, she is unapologetic in her desire for it: "It is nice. It is clean, the life Estella [Koomson] is getting" (44). And although the man insists that "some of that kind of cleanness has more rottenness in it than the slime at the bottom of a garbage dump," he admits to himself that he wishes he could provide his own family—and particularly his children—with the advantages the Koomsons enjoy (44). Unwilling to compromise his integrity but forced to recognize its cost to him and his loved ones, the man is beset by guilt, doubt, and loneliness.

The unrelenting pessimism of *Beautyful Ones* manifests itself in the novel's pervasive imagery of filth and decay, applied equally to

the supposedly "clean" lifestyle of the gleam and to the daily struggles of the masses.³ Everything the man sees or touches is unclean,
from the "rotten . . . stench" of paper money, to the waste recepta-
cle "covered over thickly with the juice of every imaginable kind of
waste matter," to the grime and stench of public restrooms (3, 7).
Even the banister in the Railroad Administration building—its
wood decaying beneath layers of polish, sullied by the traffic of
countless hands—elicits his revulsion and despair. The man is
no less revolted by his own domestic space than by these public
ones: the family's shared latrine, the shower coated with mysterious slime, and the reddish floor polish, "tired and menstrual,"
that does nothing to rejuvenate the worn surfaces to which it is
applied (118). The imagery of filth, rot, and waste in *Beautyful
Ones* is certainly not symbolically or ideologically neutral; indeed,
in Armah's text, as Joshua Esty suggests, "shit has a political voca-
tion."⁴ On the most fundamental level, these depictions contribute
to our sense of the utter degradation of the man's environment
and the daily assaults to which his values—including cleanliness
and purity—are subjected.

Falling Man offers a similarly grim view of both the present and
the future in the wake of the September 11, 2001, terrorist attacks
in New York City. DeLillo's novel steers clear of depicting the acts
of heroism and solidarity that 9/11 inspired, focusing instead on
the ordinary, banal, and even offensive reactions of flawed and fal-
lible characters. The novel's protagonist, Keith Neudecker, escapes
the Twin Towers, where several of his friends perish, but contrary
to the beatified image of the survivor that prevailed in the aftermath of 9/11, Keith is more antihero than hero. At the time of the
attacks, Keith is estranged from his wife, Lianne, and their young
son, and although the couple reunites after Keith's escape, their
relationship remains strained and distant throughout the novel.

Indeed, none of DeLillo's characters rise to the challenge articulated by Martin, a cosmopolitan art dealer and the longtime lover of Lianne's mother, Nina. In the days immediately following the attacks, Martin urges Lianne to respond rationally and productively: "There's the event, there's the individual. Measure it. Let it teach you something. See it. Make yourself equal to it" (42).

Despite Martin's advice, neither Lianne nor her mother reacts positively; indeed, Nina's unwillingness to see the events of 9/11 through the political and economic frameworks that Martin puts forward creates conflict in their long and loving relationship, and eventually leads to their separation. Lianne's initial response to 9/11, like Nina's, is dominated by incomprehension and anger. Watching the news footage of the planes, Lianne remains unable to make sense of what she sees. In the weeks and months following 9/11, she isolates herself from her friends and even incites a physical confrontation with a neighbor who plays Middle Eastern music that is audible in the halls. By the end of the novel, Lianne has turned even further inward: her volunteer work with a support group for Alzheimer's patients ends and is replaced by a private, neurotic concern with her own cognitive function; and although she begins attending church regularly, her religious experience is a profoundly solitary one.

Keith and Lianne reunite after 9/11, but their recommitment to one another takes the form of a dazed surrender rather than a conscious change. Although they agree that in "times like these, the family is necessary," the family they are able to construct together is little more than "people sharing the air" (214). Even as he recommits to his family, moreover, Keith begins an affair with a fellow survivor, Florence Givens, the owner of a briefcase he carried, in a daze, as he fled the towers. Although their relationship, with "its point of origin in smoke and fire," seems initially to offer the possibility of healing and catharsis, it quickly assumes the banal contours of an ordinary infidelity (161). "She would say what someone always says. 'Do you have to leave?' He would stand naked by the bed. 'I'll always have to leave'" (137). Keith eventually ends his relationship with Florence but remains an unreliable presence at home, traveling for days at a time to attend poker tournaments, where he plays semiprofessionally. Unlike his former regular game with a gathering of friends, these tournaments are held in generic, anonymous casinos that offer Keith a world devoid of emotional significance, where his choices are determined by the simplest principles of cause and effect. Keith's alienation and purposelessness characterize the novel's worldview: rather than presenting characters made stronger and more self-aware by the harrowing events of 9/11, or a community drawing together under duress, *Falling Man* depicts bare human survival and responses to tragedy that are anything but heroic.

The Politics of Pessimism

The grim visions that characterize both *Beautyful Ones* and *Falling Man* elicited forceful negative reactions from many of their initial readers. Leonard Kibera, for instance, disparages Armah's novel for literary shortcomings such as one-dimensional characters and lack of "development and significant plot" but is even more troubled by what he sees as Armah's "contempt for Africa."[5] Although Kibera maintains that he does not expect "moral reassurance as we grovel in the muck, nor an indication of hope contrived in desperation," he is nevertheless dissatisfied with the novel's lack of a hopeful vision.[6] Disappointed readers of DeLillo's novel offered similar critiques. The seeming prescience of much of DeLillo's previous fiction led many to embrace him as a privileged interpreter of the events of 9/11, capable of doing justice to such a momentous subject. On the publication of *Falling Man*, however, DeLillo was widely criticized for failing to provide his readers with an account of the events that offered solace, enlightenment, or transcendence. To Maureen Corrigan, reviewing the novel for National Public Radio, *Falling Man* was nothing more than "a series of gestures, some contorted, some striking, but all of them infuriatingly empty."[7] And prominent *New York Times* reviewer Michiko Kakutani was disappointed by DeLillo's choice not to center his novel on a more admirable and selfless survivor than Keith, whom she dismisses as "a self-absorbed man, who came through the fire and ash of that day and decided to spend his foreseeable future playing stupid card games in the Nevada desert."[8]

These critiques are, in essence, factually correct: Armah is contemptuous of the Ghanaian society that surrounds him, and DeLillo does focus on banality and emptiness in the wake of 9/11, rather than on the acts of heroism it inspired. But in an important sense, such responses reveal more about the expectations of readers like Kibera, Corrigan, and Kakutani, who are not merely disappointed by these novels' formal or aesthetic shortcomings but seem emotionally and even morally affronted by their pessimism. Underlying these reactions, I suggest, is an implicit sense that authors like Armah and DeLillo assume a degree of political and social responsibility in their representations of the present. Corrigan's complaint about DeLillo's "failure to deepen our understanding of September 11th" is particularly revealing: for many readers, it is not enough to merely represent 9/11; rather, it must be framed in a way that makes the events themselves meaningful within a larger social narrative.[9] And Kibera's dismay at Armah's "disaffection with the men and women of Ghana" seems to reflect his own frustrated search for a more hopeful vision of decolonization in Armah's text.[10] Indeed, the fact that these authors, writing in and about moments of crisis, do not provide redeeming narratives of transcendence or visions of social transformation is interpreted by many readers as a betrayal of some greater social responsibility.

Despite the desires and expectations that readers may bring to their fiction, *Beautyful Ones* and *Falling Man* insist that the language of hope is vulnerable to abuse, and the promise of radical social change has, to date, proved elusive. Armah's novel can be situated in relation to two significant historical moments: Ghanaian independence, in 1957, and the ouster of Kwame Nkrumah, the nation's first prime minister and president, in 1966. At the time of his election, Nkrumah was widely respected as an anticolonial leader; by the time of the coup that deposed him, however, Nkrumah's plans for the nation's economic development had proved largely unsuccessful, and his rule had become increasingly authoritarian. Although he is infrequently named in *Beautyful Ones*, Nkrumah is clearly the subject of lengthy reminiscences about an inspirational leader "grown rotten with such obscene haste" (88). As a moment of potential transformation, the 9/11 terrorist attacks differ significantly from Ghana's anticolonial struggle but similarly held the promise of inspiring a fundamental change in the life of a nation. Between 2001 and 2007, when *Falling Man* was published, however, this sense of a radical break with the past gave way to the emergence of an all-too-familiar international agenda. Rather than calling America to account as a "power that interferes, that occupies" (46), mainstream discourse used the events of 9/11 to justify new interferences and occupations, once again entangled with the profit-seeking motives of American corporations. Thus, in the contexts in which both Armah and DeLillo write, the very language of change and transformation has already proven vulnerable to exploitation, readily converted to serve conservative rather than transformative ends.

Understandably, then, both Armah and DeLillo avoid trafficking in forms of optimism that the recent past has rendered suspect. Rather than dismissing their resulting pessimism as reactionary or defeatist, however, considering these novels through the lens of dystopian literature allows us to understand their political and social engagements in slightly different terms. Although they differ in important ways from the most familiar literary dystopias, which are set in distant lands or imagined futures and frequently rely on the conventions of science fiction, both *Beautyful Ones* and *Falling Man* "offer a detailed and pessimistic presentation of the very worst of social alternatives," which Tom Moylan describes as dystopian fiction's defining attribute.[11] Dystopian literature is a genre dedicated to exposing the flaws of a given set of social conditions, and in that context, the extremely negative visions in *Beautyful Ones* and *Falling Man* enable, rather than detract from, a political critique. Indeed, the very bleakness and pessimism that readers such as Kibera, Corrigan, and Kakutani find so objectionable becomes the means through which these texts historicize oppressive conditions that might otherwise be taken for granted, thus prompting critical evaluations and opening the way for social change.

As M. Keith Booker has argued, "the principal technique of dystopian fiction is defamiliarization: by focusing their critiques of society on spatially or temporally distant settings, dystopian fictions provide fresh perspectives on problematic social and political practices that might be otherwise taken for granted or considered natural and inevitable."[12] Dystopian fiction thus offers its readers a kind of haunting double vision, an avowedly constructed fictional world that is both uncomfortably familiar and untenably alien. It is the difference of this imagined world (one in which, as in Margaret

Atwood's *Handmaid's Tale*, women can no longer control their sexual or reproductive choices, or, as in Mike Resnik's *Kirinyaga*, emigrants on a terraformed planet must live only as their Kikuyu ancestors did) that prompts readers to disavow it. But it is the similarity of such dystopian worlds, their recognizable links to the reality their authors and readers inhabit, that gives rise to their social critique. Significantly, however, both *Beautyful Ones* and *Falling Man* are set not in fantastical imagined worlds, but rather in the present or recently past social realities of their authors: Armah directly witnessed Nkrumah's rise and fall, and DeLillo, himself a resident of New York City, began his novel shortly after the 9/11 attacks. Instead of creating an alternate reality, Armah and DeLillo cultivate detachment and even disgust in order to defamiliarize the present, and the alienation that many readers experience when confronted with these novels is in fact instrumental to their production of meaningful social critiques.

For Armah, relentless, graphic scatological imagery becomes a powerful mechanism for defamiliarizing quotidian realities and pervasive ideologies. Many critics have attended to the symbolic import of Armah's depictions of excrement and the many other bodily "juices" that are central to the novel's figurative vocabulary (40). On a symbolic level, Armah's imagery evokes both the moral corruption that defines postindependence Ghanaian society and the material processes of "irresponsible consumerism and embezzlement [that] lead directly to undisposed-of filth and waste."[13] As Esty suggests, in *Beautyful Ones* "Armah uses excremental language to perform an extended Freudian unmasking or desublimation: he re-odorizes money, converting it into shit and forcing readers to see wealth as polished waste."[14] Through the effect of abjection, Armah's vivid description of waste and filth causes readers instinctively to draw back from the object, individual, or ideology with which it is associated. For instance, describing the wigs of human hair, much desired by aspiring, upwardly mobile women like Oyo, as "scraped from [a] decayed white woman's corpse" (89) accomplishes a defamiliarization that opens the familiar commodity, and its reification of colonial values, to critique. This strategy is crucial for Armah's novel, since it reveals how the man's comparatively comfortable, middle-class life, seemingly enviable at first glance, is contaminated by the internalized racism and avaricious consumerism of the society that surrounds him.

The distancing effects of DeLillo's narrative are more subtle, but no less significant. *Falling Man* invites us to see New York City in the wake of 9/11 through the eyes of a survivor, for whom familiar landscapes have become detached from their former significance. The novel's first pages describe ground zero as "not a street anymore but a world, a time and space of falling ash and near night" (3). The towers' collapse makes the ordinary scenery of the city seem strange and nonsensical: a "Breakfast Specials" sign is impossibly incongruous, and joggers stop in their tracks, their activity rendered wildly inappropriate by the enormity of the events unfolding around them (3). This sense that the familiar world has suddenly become incomprehensible was a hallmark of 9/11 discourse, especially in the weeks and months immediately following the attacks, but in DeLillo's novel, the feeling of dislocation is persistent and pervasive. The detachment of the 9/11 survivors is echoed, for example, by the Alzheimer's patients with whom Lianne conducts her "storyline sessions" (125). For these men and women, nothing about the world around them can be taken for granted, as "things fall away, streets, names, all sense of direction and location, every fixed grid of memory" (156). This sense of disconnection also suffuses DeLillo's prose, which posits the emptiness of his characters and their actions as the defining condition of an American modernity in which "individuality is rubbed out, willpower attenuated, and language barely functional."[15]

Both Armah and DeLillo, by distancing readers from their surrounding social realities, achieve the effect of cognitive estrangement that is the hallmark of dystopian fiction, calculated to generate both reflection and critique.[16] But despite their bleakness, dystopian texts are not necessarily fatalistic in their outlook, and the responses they elicit from their readers are central to determining their ideological orientation. As Tom Moylan points out, the bleakness of the imagined world in a dystopian text makes it, by definition, pessimistic. But in depicting that flawed society, a dystopian text may also suggest, directly or indirectly, that oppressive social conditions might be transformed or transcended. For Moylan, the viability of the challenge that a dystopian novel imagines largely determines the political significance of its pessimism. Thus, dystopias that prompt critical reflection on the depicted social conditions and inspire hope for a different and better alternative display "utopian pessimism," whereas those that offer no alternative to the bleak reality display "anti-utopian pessimism."[17]

On the level of plot, neither *Beautyful Ones* nor *Falling Man* imagines the possibility of a successful challenge to the current, flawed reality; indeed, both texts actively cast doubt on such a possibility. In *Beautyful Ones*, the coup deposing Nkrumah holds little promise of real or meaningful change. The man stays at his desk when his coworkers go out, opportunistically, to join demonstrations in support of the new government, and he notes that, although the words of the crowd's songs about the fallen leader have changed from praise to condemnation, the songs themselves remain the same. Nevertheless, the coup does cause one small but important change: Koomson, formerly the embodiment of everything the man had failed to achieve, is forced to flee, fearing for his life. No longer a representative of the gleam, Koomson is abjected by his fear, which produces noxious bodily odors, and he must escape from the man's house by squeezing through the narrow opening of the latrine, an image that simultaneously evokes both excretion and (re)birth. The man helps Koomson escape to safety, and Oyo, terrified and revolted by the spectacle of Koomson's fall, expresses for the first time her gratitude that her husband "never became like him" (165). Although he recognizes that the world has changed completely for individuals like Koomson, the man foresees no real change for Ghana or for himself: "for the nation itself there would only be a change of embezzlers and a change of the hunters and the hunted" (162). And reflecting on the family and the daily life to which he will always return, the man is filled not with optimism but with "the never-ending knowledge that this aching emptiness would be all that the remainder of his own life could offer him" (183).

DeLillo, too, offers very little in the way of hope, depicting the Neudecker family, years after the attacks, as locked in a pattern of rote repetition. Keith and Lianne "sink into [their] little lives," much as Keith had predicted (75). By the novel's close, they have become defined by the actions they compulsively repeat—counting by threes or going to church, playing cards or doing rehabilitative wrist exercises—actions that seem to grow more meaningless with each repetition. Keith's compulsion to correct misspellings of his last name on incoming mail, crossing out the "new" in "Neudecker," is emblematic of the novel's vision of the future, marked by empty habits that seem to foreclose the possibility of genuine change. Nina's estrangement from Martin and her eventual death also cast doubt on the possibility of the kind of personal and ideological transformation that Martin advocated in the novel's early pages. When Martin and Lianne meet for the last time, after Nina's memorial service, he has abandoned his earlier hope that Americans might rise to the challenge of seeing themselves and their place in the world differently after 9/11.

On the level of plot, then, neither *Beautyful Ones* nor *Falling Man* offers much opportunity to imagine otherwise; dismissing these texts as anti-utopian, however, overlooks the ideological implications of their form. As Moylan suggests, it is frequently the structural openness of a dystopian text, rather than its plot, that allows for hopeful and utopian possibilities. Thus, in contrast to conservative, anti-utopian texts, which "[tend] to favor a linear plot" in which all rebellions are crushed, those that offer "a possibility for change or identif[y] a site for an alternative position" allow readers to step outside of the dystopian world, critique its flaws, and imagine other, resistant possibilities.[18] Similarly, Fredric Jameson's work on utopian fiction notes the problematic nature of focusing on the content of utopian visions: inasmuch as utopian possibilities are genuinely new and different, they risk becoming "not merely unrealizable, but what is worse, unimaginable" to readers whose imaginations are shaped by their present political and social context.[19] By corollary, dystopian literature faces the opposite challenge: profoundly invested in critiquing the political and social conditions in evidence around them, dystopian texts may be unable to transcend those conditions to convincingly evoke a different and hopeful alternative. If too much difference renders utopias incomprehensible, too much sameness condemns dystopias to fatalism.

The inevitable shortcomings of the utopian imagination form the basis of the politically informed critical practice that Jameson ultimately advocates, a "utopian formalism" concerned with not only "the social and historical raw materials" from which fictional narratives are constructed, "but also the representational relations established between them—such as closure, narrative and exclusion or inversion."[20] Although utopian texts may fail to envision any genuinely different alternative to present social conditions, by making those oppressive conditions visible and allowing them to be historicized, these texts lay the groundwork for visions of the future that they themselves, by definition, may be unable to provide. Thus, as Jameson argues, "the most reliable political test [of a utopian text] lies not in any judgment on the individual work in question so much as in its capacity to generate new ones, Utopian visions that include those of the past and modify or correct them."[21]

Jameson's model calls to mind the unrealized promise of the "beautyful ones" in Armah's novel. Near the novel's close, Armah's protagonist reflects that "someday in the long future a new life would maybe flower in the country, but when it came, it would not choose as its instruments the same people who had made a habit of killing new flowers. The future goodness may come eventually, but before then where were the things in the present that would prepare the way for it?" (159–60). The imagery of flowers in this passage clearly connects it with the inscription on the bus in the final scene, from which the novel takes its title: the image of a single flower surrounded by the words "THE BEAUTYFUL ONES ARE NOT YET BORN" (183). Exemplifying Jameson's formulation, the man recognizes that "really new things" cannot emerge in the present, and turns instead to searching for "the things . . . that would prepare the way" for that as-yet-unimaginable change (159–60). Applying this model to a reading of the novels, we can imagine the possibility of "beautyful" future readers, who, like Armah's "beautyful ones," might take these novels' formal openness as the basis for utopian visions that exceed the novels' present grasp—and perhaps ours as well. Approaching *Beautyful Ones* and *Falling Man* in this way, we would look not for vibrantly imagined alternatives to the social realities the novels depict, but rather for the terrain on which readers might begin to imagine those alternatives beyond the frame of the texts themselves.

In both novels, the conditions of market capitalism—and the hollow personal relationships that the capitalist system produces—are a defining aspect of the oppressive social realities they depict. While Armah and DeLillo do not themselves offer alternatives to these dysfunctional systems, their failure to do so can be read as an invitation, especially in light of the iterative structure that defines their novels' narrative arcs. Both *Beautyful Ones* and *Falling Man* deliver their readers, at the novel's close, to a location very like its opening. At the end of Armah's novel, the man finds himself retracing, in reverse, the journey of his morning commute and witnessing for a second time the casual corruption of a bus driver. The repetition at the conclusion of *Falling Man*—a renarration of Keith's escape from the towers—is even more pronounced. By effectively beginning again, these novels carry out a repetition with a difference. Not only do their final scenes differ in subtle but important ways from the earlier versions, but we as readers approach these scenes having ourselves been transformed by the act of reading. This circular structure offers an alternative to the hopelessness and stasis that otherwise defines the novels, suggesting that change is possible and providing readers with the seeds of an alternate vision that extends forward from each novel's end.

Beginning Again

In *Beautyful Ones*, Armah's critique of Ghana's ethos of consumption is unambiguous and unrelenting; but while there is little change in the flawed society the novel depicts, its cyclical narrative offers the possibility that the man himself has changed in a subtle but important way. For much of the novel, the man tries to hold himself aloof from the corruption and materialism he denounces. In the Railroad Administration, he stubbornly refuses to acknowledge the not-so-subtle suggestions of the timber contractor who attempts to bribe him, and he avoids contaminating contact with the banister as he ascends and descends the stairs. At home and in public, the man also goes out of his way to distance himself from Oyo's social posturing, complaining to the Koomsons about the high price of even unpretentious local beer and bringing his wife abruptly down to earth during a rare taxi ride, when she flaunts "the few rich things that had ever happened to her" for the taxi driver's admiration (144). But even as he struggles to separate himself from the corrupt world around him, the man recognizes the futility of doing so. He recalls a friend, Rama Krishna, a Ghanaian man who took that name in his search for spiritual purity, whose efforts to avoid contamination were even more extreme. "Near the end he had discovered the one way: he would not corrupt himself by touching any woman, but saved his semen to rejuvenate his brain by standing on his head a certain number of minutes every night and every dawn" (48). Despite his ascetic quest to keep his body and mind pure, Rama Krishna dies of consumption, his body having "undergone far more decay than any living body, however old and near death, can expect to see" (48–49).

Rama Krishna's story points to the sexual, as well as financial, dimensions of the idealized purity that the man and others around him seek. Throughout Armah's novel, the normative gender roles that cast men as providers and women as consumers forge a powerful link between the economic and sexual failings of men like the novel's protagonist. Indeed, it comes as little surprise that the man, who has no appetite for the national game of corruption and social climbing, has also lost his sexual appetite for his wife and has no money to pay for the services of the prostitute who propositions him during Passion Week. In his attempt to resist the prevailing social forces, the man feels burdened by Oyo's hopes and aspirations and yearns for a solitary life like that of the man he calls "Teacher," who has "escaped the call of the loved ones" (55). For Teacher, as for the man, the expectations and desires of women—mothers, wives, and lovers—weigh heavily: despite his love for Maanan, in her presence Teacher feels "accused by a silence that belonged to millions and ages of women all bearing the face and the form of Maanan, and needing no voice at all to tell me I had failed them" (72).[22] Although the man describes Teacher as "the freest person I know" (55), Teacher's account of his own loneliness suggests that neither option—disappointing loved ones or living without them—holds much promise of happiness.

To justify his solitude and withdrawal from public life, Teacher cites Plato's allegory of the cave: people imprisoned in the dark, who have seen only a reflection of the sun, refuse to believe the account of one among them who has witnessed the brightness of daylight. For Teacher, the parable captures the futility of struggling for change in a postindependence Ghana whose citizens are so seduced by the false values of consumer capitalism that they reject other visions for the nation's future out of hand. In his despair, Teacher concludes, in the spirit of Plato, that "men were all free to do what they chose to do, and would laugh at the bringer of unwanted light if they knew what they needed was the dark" (79). When he hears this story, the man is saddened but convinced by it. But Teacher's interpretation of the allegory ignores one of its defining features: the conditions of imprisonment that cause the prisoners in the cave to doubt the escapee's visionary claim. This is the aspect of the allegory that John Lutz emphasizes in his reading of the novel, which recasts Armah's pessimism in an explicitly Marxist framework. If, as Lutz suggests, "those imprisoned in the cave are understood primarily as prisoners of social desire who have been miseducated in a way that makes them incapable of recognizing what is in their own best interests," the parable directs our attention to the fundamental changes that would need to occur before the prisoners could, literally, see the light.[23] Both the allegory and Teacher's deployment of it neglect the point on which the man ultimately focuses: the conditions in the present that will prepare the way for future change.

The conclusion of *Beautyful Ones* is ambivalent at best. The conditions are no different in the Ghana to which the man returns after his adventure with Koomson: desperate children still steal chips of stone from grave markers, and officials still casually demand bribes. But unlike Teacher, who is determined to hold himself apart from that world, the man has chosen to engage with it. He has risked his life to help Koomson, compromising his own principles to help the party man bribe his way to safety. And while Teacher cannot bring himself to speak to Maanan and acknowledge his failings and her suffering, the man, encountering Maanan on the beach, calls her by name in a gesture of recognition. Although he dreads returning to "Oyo, [and] the eyes of the children after six o'clock," the man nevertheless sets off toward home at the novel's close (183). After bribing the soldiers at a roadblock while the man looks on, the driver of the green bus with its hopeful inscription waves and smiles to the man as he drives off, hailing him much as the man hailed Maanan.

The man's reaction to the driver's gesture is ambiguous, and critics such as Robert Spencer have suggested that this interaction, in which the man is once again a passive watcher of the corruption around him, confirms his aloofness and isolation.[24] But read alongside the account of the bus journey that begins the novel, this scene suggests an important shift in the man's attitude and outlook. In the earlier scene, the man is literally asleep with his eyes open, seeming to stare in judgment as the bus driver counts the day's take, and the man's perceived refusal to condone the graft enrages the driver. In the later scene, the man's response to the bus driver is not described, but the driver's friendly attitude suggests an important difference in how his watching has been perceived. As Neil Lazarus suggests, "the bus-driver sees the watching 'man' not as a stern figure of conscience, calling him to account, nor—of course—as a partner in crime, but as one who understands."[25] While the subtle change that the man has undergone over the course of the novel is not explicitly described in the text, it is revealed by this cyclical structure, which allows us to see the earlier scene repeated, but with a difference. Armah's text does not imagine any viable alternatives to the man's bleak existence, and the hopeful readings offered by critics often seem more definitive than the novel's ending warrants. But the novel does suggest the possibility that the future might differ from the present we have witnessed, a possibility embodied by the green bus. In the context of a dystopian world in which "all that can be expected from the present is that it will not foreclose every single one of the future's progressive options," the fact that the man is open to this promise is itself a form of hope.[26]

Similarly, throughout *Falling Man*, DeLillo grapples with the fact that the American way of life under attack on 9/11 was defined by the oppressive conditions of late capitalism, conditions that he has critiqued extensively in his earlier fiction. Like the coup in Armah's novel, which yields simply "a change of embezzlers" (162), 9/11 only superficially alters life for the Neudecker family; they remain isolated and adrift in the modern world they occupy.

Although Keith survives and the family is reunited, the novel suggests that the normal lives they try to re-create are defined by an empty, alienating consumer capitalism. Keith's transformation from financier to professional poker player simply substitutes one form of empty, fetishistic financial dealing for another. And throughout *Falling Man*, even the most basic activities are mechanized and dehumanized. To do laundry, Lianne must first "make selections on the control panel, set the dial on the other side of the panel and close the lid" in a laundry room with a "metallic chill that she felt in her teeth" (150). At the bakery, she must "take a number from the dispenser on the counter"; as she waits, she realizes that "she hated this regimen of assigned numbers, strictly enforced, in a confined space, with nothing at the end of the process but a small white bow-tied box of pastry" (36). In scenes such as these, DeLillo emphasizes the alienating effects of American late capitalism, social conditions that are revealed, but not meaningfully altered, by the events of 9/11.

The personal relationships in DeLillo's novel are also profoundly marked by the effects of capitalist alienation. One of the most intimate moments readers witness in the brief affair between Keith and Florence takes place at Macy's, where Florence has come to purchase a mattress. In this scene, the private space of the bedroom is transformed into the commercial space of the mattress department, and DeLillo fetishistically repeats brand names like "Beautyrest" and "Posturepedic" that evoke a corporatized and consumption-based domesticity (132). As Florence tests her mattress, Keith surveys the room and sees other shoppers doing the same, including a couple, "middle-aged and purposeful, trying to determine whether one person's tossing would disturb the other's sleep" (132). "Bouncing and rolling," the men and women in the mattress department perform their sleep in public, eroding the significance of this private, intimate act (132). In a similar moment, during the early stages of their reconciliation, Keith and Lianne make out in the back of a taxi, and Lianne thinks to herself, "*it's a movie, it's a movie,*" their real-life intimacy somehow stranger and less familiar than images on a screen (104). Later, when Keith travels to poker tournaments, their intimate relations become even more mediated and mechanical: he and Lianne have phone sex, separated by several time zones, and in her absence, she imagines him having "automated teller sex" with a call girl (233).

Through these meaningless actions and hollow relationships, *Falling Man* calls into question any celebratory notion of the American way of life that Islamic fundamentalism has placed under attack. Within the novel, it is Martin who gives voice to this critique, suggesting that America is defined by little more than its role as a global economic superpower. If the September 11 attacks mark the end of that era of dominance, Martin contends, they only reveal the emptiness underlying America's national identity. "Soon the day is coming when nobody has to think about America except for the danger it brings. It is losing the center. It becomes the center of its own shit" (191). Although Nina's former colleagues, whom Martin is addressing, take umbrage at his statements, they do not contest his central claim that America has been defined by its role as an economic superpower. "Ask yourself," they challenge him, "what comes after America?" (192). Martin's response, that "there is an empty space where America used to be," eerily echoes the logic of DeLillo's terrorists (193). The character Hammad, the ingenuous young jihadist, asks a similar question of Amir, DeLillo's representation of so-called 9/11 mastermind Mohamed Atta: "What of the others, those who will die?" Amir responds that "there are no others. The others exist only to the degree that they fill the role we have designed for them" (176), an assertion uncomfortably similar to the larger logic of DeLillo's novel. Hammad comes to accept this explanation, musing that "these people, what they hold so precious we see as empty space" (177). Although they reflect profoundly different ideologies and motives, Martin's and Hammad's statements both suggest that in an America so pervasively shaped by late capitalism, there is nothing of value to either preserve or destroy.

This nihilistic outlook is reflected in the first account of Keith's escape from the Twin Towers, with which the novel begins. Keith is alone as he emerges onto the street, surrounded by swirling, meaningless scraps of the corporate world: "the paper massed in the air, contracts, resumés blowing by, intact snatches of business, quick in the wind" (4). Amid this debris, the image of a falling shirt stands out; in this scene, the shirt is empty, "lifted and drifting in the scant light and then falling again, down toward the river" (4). The falling shirt has particular significance in light of the many victims who fell or jumped from the towers' higher floors, a fact that the novel's title brings powerfully to mind. In this first scene, however, the "falling man" is revealed to be only an empty shirt. This scene seems to suggest that much of what was destroyed on 9/11—contracts and resumés, white shirts, and perhaps even Keith himself—was already empty long before the towers fell.

By narrating Keith's escape a second time, however, the novel creates an opportunity for readers to understand it in new terms. As Keith and Lianne watch the news footage of the attacks, they model a similar transformation for the novel's readers: "It still looks like an accident, the first one," Keith reflects, watching the impact of the first plane. "But only the first. . . . The second plane, by the time the second plane appears, . . . we're all a little older and wiser" (135). Like Keith and Lianne, we are older and wiser by the time we arrive at the second account of Keith's survival, which concludes the novel. The two accounts are factually consistent, but the second version is longer and more complete, beginning with Keith inside his office, where he witnesses the death of his friend Rumsey, and then describing his long, slow descent of the stairs with the other survivors. By this time, we have gleaned details from the novel's preceding pages that give us deeper insight into Keith's experience, allowing us to construct a more hopeful interpretation of these events than the novel itself explicitly provides.

Readers of the novel come to know Rumsey through Keith's memories of him—a nebbishy, balding man whom we eventually realize is one of Keith's few true friends. Hardly a heroic character, Rumsey is a man whose many flaws and compulsions, together with his unflinching honesty about them, endear him to Keith, and their friendship occasions rare moments of sincerity in the superficial world the novel depicts: "The persistence of the man's needs had a kind of crippled appeal. It opened Keith to dimmer things, at odder angles, to something crouched and uncorrectable in people but also capable of stirring a warm feeling in him, a rare tinge of affinity" (123). The closeness of the friendship between Keith and Rumsey, though never explicitly stated, profoundly informs our reading of the second account of Keith's escape. In the second account, Rumsey is everywhere, and the fact of Keith's survival contrasts powerfully with that of Rumsey's death. As others in his office move toward the exits, Keith looks for Rumsey, who has already been gravely injured by falling debris. As he attempts to lift Rumsey and carry him to safety, Keith sees "something outside, going past the window," the image of a "man falling sideways, arm out and up" (242, 244). Rumsey dies moments later, a fact that Keith only partially apprehends; flashing back to this moment as he descends the stairs, Keith conflates his friend in his memory with the falling man: "For an instant he saw it again, going past the window, and this time he thought it was Rumsey" (244).

Later, when he sees firefighters heading up the stairs, he thinks again of Rumsey and is reassured by the illogical belief that they will carry him to safety.

By narrating Keith's escape a second time, DeLillo allows readers to reevaluate Keith's seeming isolation and emotional distance in earlier scenes. His poker playing, in particular, takes on new meaning in light of his grief over Rumsey's death. Juxtaposing Keith's fragmentary memories of Rumsey with his desire for the "crucial anonymity" of the Las Vegas tournaments, his poker playing becomes not an empty, alienating act, but rather a desperate attempt to keep the painful memory of his lost friend at bay (204). "I heard he went out a window, Rumsey," recalls Terry Cheng (205), a mutual acquaintance and fellow poker player, whose comment, like Keith's seemingly impassive response, takes on new meaning in light of the novel's final scene. Staring into the casino's artificial waterfall, Keith is not so much embracing the artificiality of his environment as managing his powerful emotions; he stares at the waterfall because "if he closed his eyes, he'd see something" (205). The intensity of Keith's grief in this scene attests to the powerful bond he shared with Rumsey, who is far more than the mere "buddy" that the novel initially describes (22). Their caring relationship offers an alternative to the detached, unfeeling masculinity that the novel attributes to Keith, a man who is never able to grow into the role of safe, domestic provider and "husbandman" that his wife imagines for him (70).

In a similar way, understanding the life-saving role of Florence's briefcase allows us to reevaluate the relationship between Florence and Keith, which on the surface seems pathetically empty and predictable. The second account of Keith's escape transforms the earlier imagery of meaningless debris into deeply personal objects: Rumsey's shattered coffee cup, still held in his hand, a child's tricycle carried by a stranger, and a briefcase that we recognize as Florence's, although it is never explicitly identified as such. During his descent, we learn, Keith stops midway and cannot be persuaded to continue until someone hands him a briefcase dropped by its owner; taking up the briefcase and completing the comprehensible task of carrying it down the stairs, Keith is finally able to continue out of the building to safety. At the time, Keith does not know Florence—he meets her later, when he sets out to return the briefcase to its owner—but readers recognize the briefcase from the memories that Keith and Florence have shared with one another in previous scenes. The significance of the moment on the stairs goes unmarked in the text, but as readers we realize that Florence's briefcase has just saved Keith's life. This recognition, made possible by the novel's cyclical structure, recasts Florence's earlier confession that Keith "saved [her] life" by returning her briefcase (108). Although Florence's statement initially seems like the desperate hyperbole of a neglected lover, the revelation that Keith, in turn, has been indirectly saved by Florence suggests a more reciprocal connection between them. In place of the oppressive gender roles their relationship seemed to reproduce—the needy, passive woman and the detached, decisive man—we are able to reimagine a more meaningful and sustaining connection that transcends their socially scripted roles as participants in a failed extramarital affair.

Ultimately, *Falling Man*'s cyclical structure brings us to an ending point that is also the starting point for a reevaluation of the entire novel, one in which isolation and emotional distance are replaced by intimacy, reciprocity, and profound grief. The novel's final image, the falling shirt, returns us to the opening scene, but with its symbolism entirely transformed. The previously empty shirt is now personified, its "*arms* waving like nothing in this life" (246), attesting to the human significance of the destruction that took place on 9/11. In effect, this scene allows us as readers to begin the novel again with a changed understanding. Without invalidating the novel's earlier critique, it gives readers a chance to imagine an alternative to the emptiness that most of the novel depicts. The World Trade Center towers become, in addition to "fantasies of wealth and power that would one day become fantasies of destruction" (116), the locus for meaningful, defining human relationships that resist the alienating effects of the late capitalist society around them. Objects like a shirt or a briefcase can have incalculable value in their human dimension. And Keith is no longer the kind of man who would "break up a table and burn it so he could take out his dick and piss on the flames" (104), whose masculine identity precludes meaningful, intimate bonds with women and men alike. The depth and intimacy of Keith's relationship with Rumsey offers an alternative to the socially normative forms of masculinity that the novel depicts, and his bond with Florence transcends its sexual dimension, providing a counterpoint to the one-sided, "automated teller sex" in which men like Keith are expected to engage (233). These interpretations are not explicit in DeLillo's text, but are enabled by a rereading or reconsideration of the novel in light of its final scene. Ultimately, *Falling Man*'s repetitive structure challenges the nihilism of Martin and the terrorists and lays the groundwork for an alternative to the bleak, alienated social landscape it depicts—an alternative that can serve as the basis for a different vision of post-9/11 America.

Ghostly Forms of Hope

Analyzing the ways in which *Beautyful Ones* and *Falling Man* open themselves to rereading and reinterpretation highlights a dimension of these works' political and social engagements that is marginalized by a focus on the content of the bleak realities they depict. Although neither explicitly envisions viable alternatives, their use of structural repetition invites readers to pick up where the texts themselves leave off, suggesting that the process of reading might itself be the source of new and more hopeful possibilities that these works and their authors cannot yet presage. What does it look like, then, to read these two novels today, either a decade or a half-century distant from the historical moments in which they were written? In an important sense, we can no longer read either *Beautyful Ones* or *Falling Man* today as their original readers did; even if we lived through the events and eras they capture, we read them now in retrospect. To some extent, therefore, our present perspective diminishes the shock value of these works' dystopian vision; with hindsight, their grim predictions may have come to seem inevitable. This is, indeed, the kind of distorted retrospection that Jennifer Wenzel identifies in narratives of the Third World that presume the failures of decolonization to be inevitable and, in doing so, erase decisive moments when history could have unfolded differently.[27] While a retrospective position may be inescapable, however, it need not be reactionary; it could in fact be transformative. To the extent that these works invite rereading, their dystopian form may enable us to read them differently, perhaps even to envision the kinds of hopeful possibilities that exceeded the grasp of their initial readers.

If we can no longer encounter these works as their initial readers did, are we now the "beautyful" future readers who will be able take their structural openness as the basis for imagining a future that is radically—unfathomably—different from the worlds these works depict? I think not. The United States is still fighting the wars that 9/11 was used to justify, and will be for the foreseeable future. And Ghana, still burdened by the social and political legacies of colonization and underdevelopment, is praised by the West as a "stable democracy" in the context of its government's decision, against public outcry, to accept the transfer of two detainees from the American military prison at Guantanamo Bay.[28] In an important sense, the world we live in today may not have changed in appreciable ways from what Armah and DeLillo describe in their respective novels. But it is precisely this lack of change that demonstrates the value of these novels' formal politics: their structural openness continues to allow for hopeful possibilities that, while not yet realized in the present, are not invalidated by it, either. Quite the opposite of the "fragile" texts that Peter Rabinowitz describes, which can be irreversibly damaged through certain acts of reading, *Beautyful Ones* and *Falling Man* employ narrative and aesthetic mechanisms that make them fundamentally resilient: if we are not yet these novels' "beautyful" readers, the spaces for rereading and reinterpretation from which hopeful interpretations might emerge remain open for readers of the future.[29] Even a term like "resilience," of course, is not without its ironies; at the time of this writing, resilience is having a moment, touted by governments and corporations in response to the threat of future global—frequently ecological—catastrophes they are unwilling to avert and therefore frame as inevitable.[30] In writing about the future, it seems, my language is no less vulnerable to co-optation or inversion than Armah's or DeLillo's.

It's no accident that the structure of these two novels is one of journey and return: like Sethe in her bed and Puran boarding his bus, like Ammu and Velutha on the riverbank and Tayo greeting the sunrise, like Ed Horman flying home and Gamini committedly remaining there, hauntings return us, changed, to the place where we began. As works of fiction that haunt us with our own as-yet-unrealized possible futures, *The Beautyful Ones Are Not Yet*

Born and *Falling Man* offer us, with each reading, an opportunity to return to the beginning. By the end of these works, we're invited to see that seemingly static repetition is in fact dynamic and can reveal at least the possibility of change: traces of choice and agency become visible in the man's grudging acceptance of his daily routine, and the grief that suffuses *Falling Man* suggests that survivors like Keith and Lianne might at some point begin to heal. While we, as readers of these novels, may not yet be able to imagine alternatives to the bleak realities they depict, their future readers might be. But haunting also teaches us that anything truly different—including futures—resists being known; only by relinquishing the desire to know the future, then, do we leave ourselves open to the possibility of encountering it.

Conclusion

ON DREAM FISH AND THE
LIMITS OF FICTION

"If you eat fish in a dream, does it count? Does it mean you've eaten fish?" (*God of Small Things*, 208). In many ways, the ethical concerns at the heart of this book hinge on the answer we give to Estha's and Rahel's question. What does it mean for an experience—like eating fish, or happiness—to feel real? In other words, how do the contents of imagined worlds bear on the reality we inhabit?

I've never dreamed about fish, but I have made myself macaroni after reading the scene in *A Farewell to Arms* when Fred Henry brings food to his ambulance drivers at the front; and Desdemona Stephanides's pleasure at soaking her aging feet in Jeffrey Eugenides's *Middlesex* has inspired me to draw a bath. In recounting these fleeting intersections between the fictional world and the real one, I'm embarrassed by both their literalness and their smallness. As a literature professor who zealously reminds my students that the fictional worlds they've inhabited while reading are not real, I of all people should know better than to map the fictional world so directly onto my own reality. Making macaroni after reading about macaroni, in this context, seems unforgivably naïve. Indeed, if Freud has taught us nothing else, it's that the contents of our dreams are obscured, occulted, and fundamentally symbolic; by that logic, what the fish-eating dreamer of Roy's novel really wants to do is probably better left to the imagination. What's more, focusing on such concrete, peripheral details of these fictional worlds seems utterly banal in the context of the larger stories these works tell. Desdemona's foot bath is entirely tangential to the main action of the scene in which it occurs, a reconciliation between grandmother and grandson, and few readers are likely to even remember it. Similarly, Fred Henry's concern with his men's dinner at the front tells us something important about his character, and their meal immediately precedes a harrowing artillery attack that nearly costs Fred his life and fundamentally changes his views on the war. The macaroni is hardly the point.

I share these experiences because I suspect they can't be all that uncommon, even among those of us supposedly savvy readers who think and write about books for a living. This is, after all, how fiction is supposed to work—inspiring us to conjure up fictional people, places, and things through imaginative processes that draw on the sensory and emotional raw materials of our own lived experience. But like Roy's distinction between dream fish and real fish, these stories also graphically illustrate the incommensurability of the fictional and nonfictional worlds. I don't have Desdemona's aging feet, and I'm not braving artillery fire in the First World War, so the actions of soaking or eating macaroni mean something substantially different when I do them; I engage in these activities not in order to feel close to the fictional characters who inspire them, but because in my present reality I anticipate that they will be pleasurable or rewarding. These examples, then, attest to both the potential linkages between real and imagined worlds, and the persistence of the gap between them; in that gap, where narrative form interacts in complex and potentially unpredictable ways with the readerly imagination, is where rhetorical narrative theory resides.

In a well-known cartoon by Sidney Harris, two mathematicians consider a proof on a chalkboard, an intermediate step of which states, "then a miracle occurs"; the caption reads, "I think you should be more explicit here in step two."[1] As literary critics, who recognize the constructedness of fictional texts but nevertheless believe that they matter in the wider world, we find ourselves in a similar situation: although we are confident that fiction and reality are linked, the precise mechanism by which we move from one to the other can be difficult to identify. Defining the nature of that connection—and, in essence, answering Estha's and Rahel's question—requires us to attend to the complex interactions between readers and texts: to the properties of storytelling that make our experiences of fictional worlds feel real, and those that, like the dream fish and real fish in the twins' question, call our attention to their incommensurability. As I hope to have shown, a rhetorical understanding of how fiction works with and on its readers provides valuable insights into that undefined space where texts, through the act of reading, become consequential in the wider world. Bringing the concepts and methods of rhetorical narrative theory to bear on works like the ones I consider here, which reach their readers across boundaries of national and cultural difference, in turn, offers valuable insights into some of the most abiding ethical questions that arise from the study of ethnic and Third World literature.

As the readings in each of the preceding chapters demonstrate, attending to the ways that narrative forms interact with readers' desires and expectations can productively complicate and enrich the purely linguistic model that has long held sway in ethnic and postcolonial studies. These fields, whose flourishing in the academy in the last decades of the twentieth century accompanied the so-called linguistic turn, have overwhelmingly embraced poststructuralist principles that credit the text itself with an un-precedented power to shape, rather than passively reflect, existing realities. This is the logic behind the widespread concern with the politics of representation, as I suggested at the beginning of this book: if texts shape reality, the act of representing, in and of itself, becomes materially consequential. In making this link between fiction and reality, poststructuralist theory privileges difference, frequently in the guise of the so-called "otherness postmodern-ism" that Sue J. Kim so acutely critiques.[2] As Kim points out, how-ever, the conceit that the alterity of the text inherently generates an oppositional politics is ultimately not borne out by fact. Despite such limitations, however, the ongoing debate about how best to study and read world literature continues to be framed most often along these lines, in primarily linguistic terms.

Although the fundamental questions at the heart of this debate—about the artistic, intellectual, and ethical stakes of reading globally and cross-culturally—remain urgent and profoundly consequen-tial, the debate itself frequently takes on the frustratingly circular quality of an academic turf war. The polarization and combative tone that have characterized the world literature debate derive in large part, I want to suggest, from its reliance on poststructural-ist understandings of literature's relationship to reality, which, like Kim's otherness postmodernism, overstate the power of the text itself, while obscuring the mechanisms through which it actually comes to have effects in the wider world. Scholars on both sides of this debate presuppose a straightforward analogy between tex-tual structures and social relations: if we make texts broadly acces-sible through circulation and translation, we bring people together, whereas if we insist on untranslatability and the need for specialist knowledge, we protect fragile literatures and cultures from being appropriated by an expansionist Western academy.

In this way, then, the world literature debate breaks down, in basic terms, to a methodological contest between generality and specificity. On the side of generality are the proponents of World Literature as a discipline, in the sense proposed initially by Goethe and championed in a variety of related forms by scholars like David Damrosch, Pascale Casanova, Franco Moretti, and Rebecca Walkowitz.[3] In this model, we should value works for their ability to travel and become meaningful in a wide range of contexts beyond the one in which they were created. For Damrosch, the category of world literature is itself expansive and could be taken to include "all works that circulate beyond their culture of origin, either in translation or in their original language."[4] By this definition, a text's formal or thematic features may predispose it to being read broadly, but it is taken up and put into global circulation by its readers and critics; indeed, a work's status as world literature may vary according to time and place. In advancing this definition, Damrosch maintains that translation (both linguistic and cultural) is intellectually fruitful and adequate to the task of revealing those elements of a text's meaning that transcend its original context; indeed, works of world literature gain through their circulation, adding layers of significance as they travel and remaining available for meaning-making despite the inevitable losses or transformations that process of circulation entails. In a similar way, Franco Moretti's controversial interest in literary networks or systems, rather than the particularities of close reading, proceeds from the proposition that large-scale analysis can reveal surprising and persuasive linkages that more narrowly focused approaches cannot.[5]

Skeptics of this model worry, first and foremost, that it sacrifices the analytical precision of attending to distinct literary and linguistic forms or specific historical and cultural contexts—in effect, that it authorizes a kind of sloppy reading. Contained within such arguments against promiscuous literary travel, however, lurks a not-so-subtle concern with questions of aesthetic or imaginative propriety: a fear that certain kinds of readers might read inappropriately. Indeed, the evocative term for what critics of World Literature most fear—"McDonaldization"—makes it clear that we're dealing not only with matters of power but also of taste: if texts travel too freely along global circuits of exchange, the particularities of literary forms, like the local cuisines supplanted by the now-ubiquitous fast food chain, might be not only homogenized but also debased to appeal to economically powerful but regrettably unsophisticated American palates. So I sympathize with Damrosch when he calls attention to the elitism that often lies behind such objections, which make deep linguistic and historical knowledge a prerequisite to reading works from cultures other than one's own: isn't some exposure to world literature, even in a compromised form, better than none at all?[6] But like Puran, who worries that when stories about Pirtha circulate out of context, "the rodent and the rhododendron will be proven the same" ("Pterodactyl," 162), I also recognize that meanings become unstable across boundaries of difference, and that such instability opens the possibility of misunderstanding and even abuse.

If, at one pole of the debate, World Literature risks flattening difference, Comparative Literature, on the other, celebrates cultural specificity, aesthetic particularity, and the residue of the untranslatable that persists in the spaces between languages and cultures, marking the place where meaning-making reaches its limits. For Emily Apter, both translation and untranslatability—which she calls "a linguistic form of creative failure"—together are the constitutive elements of world literary forms.[7] Only by attending to those spaces where meaning is insistently local and recalcitrantly particular can translation retain its integrity; she cites Barbara

Cassin's *Dictionary of Untranslatables* as exemplifying the principles of "a translational humanities whose fault lines traverse the cultural subdivisions of nations or 'foreign' languages by coalescing around hubs of singularity."[8] This investment in incommensurability, which animates Apter's practice of translation, is what Damrosch notably misconstrues in his conversation with Gayatri Spivak at the 2011 meeting of the American Comparative Literature Association, taking her investment in singularity as a desire to study texts or authors singly.[9] On the contrary, for Spivak, as for Apter, singularity—the condition of ethical responsibility that derives from insuperable difference—necessarily lies at the heart of comparison. Only by recognizing the absolute alterity of the other, Spivak insists, can we enter into any form of ethical relation; this is equally true of people and of literary forms. Similarly, then, in Apter's account of Cassin, the unifying "hubs" around which translation coalesces are not those sites where translation succeeds (as they would be for Damrosch), but rather, the places where it fails.

For comparativists like Spivak and Apter, then, particularism is the enabling condition of an ethical cross-culturalism, even—or especially—when it gives rise to noncommunication or aporia. Indeed, as I've shown throughout this book, the textual features that, through their irreducible complexity and ambiguity, resist being put into interpretive circulation, serve very constructively to mitigate against misreading when literary works from the margins enter into broad circulation. But it's also this same quality of unyieldingness that makes me wince when well-intentioned readers, inspired by a sincere desire to understand more about marginalized literatures and the historical and cultural contexts from which they arise, unintentionally select some of the least accessible works I study and teach to serve as their introduction. There are valid reasons, beyond mere expediency, to pick a novel like Chimamanda

Ngozi Adichie's *Americanah*, rather than one like Gayl Jones's *Corregidora*, to introduce an unfamiliar reader to the literature of the African diaspora. Jones's novel is quite intentionally difficult to read, and it does not diminish its value or importance to suggest that it does little to inform—or transform—the reader who cannot bear to finish it. While difference may be necessary to any ethics of reading, there is value in the substrate of sameness that makes communication and emotional engagement possible—the kind of contact and recognition that I have been calling, in the context of this project, an encounter.

Clearly, both generalizing and particularizing frameworks offer important insights into the ways literary texts circulate beyond their countries and cultures of origin; but both frameworks, inevitably, have their limitations. This commonsense acknowledgement can seem almost impossible in the context of the world literature debate, which positions these two approaches in adversarial opposition to one another. The roots of this particularly stubborn disagreement, I believe, lie in the logic of the linguistic turn, which overstates the inherent power of literary language to embody an ethical position. If the language of fiction in and of itself has the property of being ethical (rather than generating or inspiring ethical action on the part of its readers), scholarly methodologies that either illuminate or overlook the specific features credited with embodying that ethics (either translatability or untranslatability) take on greater significance. The result, then, are pitched debates that position generality and particularity as irreconcilable opposites, and in which the stakes are nothing less than honoring or vacating the text's ethical force.

The so-called affective turn, therefore, is in part a reaction against the seeming sterility of the poststructuralist privileging of language, one that might offer a more productive model of how fiction becomes consequential in the wider world: not through the world-making power of language, but instead through the embodied, visceral responses of readers. For Sianne Ngai, for instance, "ugly feelings" in literature speak not only to the social dilemmas of characters like Melville's Bartleby the scrivener, but also to the larger "question of relevance . . . that has often haunted the discipline of literary and cultural criticism."[10] Indeed, in a certain sense, attention to affect in the study of world literature predates the broader critical groundswell of the affective turn. Fellow feeling is the property that underwrites the logic of cosmopolitanism, as advanced most prominently by someone like Kwame Anthony Appiah, in which our sense of affective connection with others supplants moral prescriptions (or legal protections) as the basis for treating others with tolerance and compassion.[11]

Like most correctives, there's value and insight in the turn to affect; first and foremost, in the context of this study's concerns, it reinscribes readers as the object or recipient of literature's representational effects. But approaches that promote affect—like those that elevate the alterity of the text—as de facto drivers of narrative ethics ultimately provide similar cause for concern. As a hinge between real and imagined worlds, affect is unpredictable: my own experience making macaroni illustrates that the link that affect forges between reader and text is not necessarily a politically significant one. Brian Massumi is right to remind us that affect, like post-structuralist alterity, is not automatically political. It is rather, as he suggests, "proto-political": "It concerns the first stirrings of the political, flush with the felt intensities of life," but "its politics must be brought out."[12] While affect may spark political awareness and lead to concrete social action, it need not do so. Indeed, as Bruce Robbins points out, "global feeling," the spirit of human fellowship that summons allegiances and projects ethical obligation beyond the proximate, is not qualitatively different from "national feeling," but rather "an extension outward of the same sorts of potent and dangerous solidarity."[13] While affect can be powerful, then, it can also be unruly, and as these examples suggest, it can be elicited or directed in various ways, some more desirable than others.

Ultimately, approaches to the study of world literature that privilege either language or affect paint an incomplete picture of literature's relationship to the social world: assuming that language in and of itself can be inherently ethical effaces real people as ethical agents, while focusing on readers' affects potentially decouples affective responses from the concrete formal features that inspire them. At the risk of oversimplification, then, we can imagine that language and affect exist on opposite sides of our cartoon mathematicians' blackboard; neither can fully account for the miraculous second step by which textual forms give rise to real-world effects. Rhetorical narrative theory, which attends in precise and demonstrable ways to the dynamic interaction between reader and text, is especially well suited to this task. In the preceding chapters, I have endeavored to shed light on these dynamic interactions—the forces that draw readers into fictional worlds, as well as those that push them away. Indeed, thinking of the mimetic and metafictional strategies these works employ as forces underscores the particular insight that rhetorical narrative theory provides: these narrative effects are generated by specific formal features, and they act on their objects—readers—in ways that are recognizable but also complex and not necessarily predictable. If the pull of Devi's mimetic account of the pterodactyl is weaker than my resistance to her novella's supernatural conceit, for instance, I won't be affected to the same degree as a reader more willing to suspend her disbelief. In similar ways, all the works I've examined here actively negotiate between closeness and distance, employing narrative strategies that shape, but never fully determine, the dynamics of their global circulation; it's on this basis, I contend, that they should be considered works of world literature.

Throughout this book, I've offered haunting as a model for understanding the ethical encounters between world fiction and its readers at a distance. Each work demonstrates, in its own way, that fiction has the power to stage encounters with the inhabitants of other worlds, but insists that these intense, temporary encounters take place across necessary boundaries of difference. When Sethe and Puran nurture ghostly visitors, but must move forward without them; when writers like Roy or Silko tell carefully crafted stories of trauma; when victims of disappearance are conjured through fiction; and when ghostly visions of a transformed future are both offered and withheld—these fictional maneuvers negotiate productively between sameness and difference. Facing the twin imperatives of forging connections with readers and marking the limits of such imaginative traffic, these works stage complex negotiations that balance these two competing aims. Through an analysis grounded in rhetorical narrative theory, I have shown that the works examined here, and many others like them, are not the passive objects of circulation and interpretation, but rather anticipate and respond to the conditions that allow them to reach readers across boundaries of cultural difference. Through their underlying narrative infrastructure, these works balance the sense of sameness necessary to feel implicated in another's story with the recognition of difference that resists colonizing that other's experience with one's own.

Recognizing that narrative forms are responsible for producing and directing the ethical engagements of their readers does not absolve us, as literary critics, of responsibility for assessing the ethical implications of specific texts or acts of reading; nor does it imply that all works of world literature are ethically equivalent. In different ways, each of the works considered here falls short of its ethical ideal, and it's easy to think of others with deeper flaws or more pernicious intents. But by examining the dynamic interactions between readers and texts—and in particular, the ways that certain works have the power to haunt us—we can better understand how and why fiction becomes ethical: we can credit literary language for its prodigious world- and idea-making properties, and we can appropriately value our affective responses to works that are intended to affect us. This assertion advances from the seemingly straightforward premise that works of literature become ethical through acts of reading. Attending to these ethical dynamics, in the end, means acknowledging what we've always at some level known: that eating fish in a dream is not the same as eating fish. For good or for ill, books are just books; people are the ones who act ethically toward one another in ways that matter. This recognition, to me, both inspires humility and offers reassurance: fiction can make us think and feel, but we're the ones who ultimately decide how to act.

Notes

Introduction

1. Devi, "Pterodactyl, Puran Sahay, and Pirtha," 196.
2. Freud, "The Uncanny."
3. Derrida, *Specters of Marx*.
4. Kathleen Brogan, in *Cultural Haunting*, interprets the recurring theme of haunting in contemporary ethnic literature through the lens of contested cultural memory. Reflecting a substantially different set of investments, Avery Gordon, *Ghostly Matters*, meditates on haunting as the lingering trace of historical, cultural, and methodological erasures.
5. Questions about representation lie at the heart of foundational works by scholars including Stuart Hall, Gayatri Spivak, Edward Said, Henry Louis Gates Jr., and bell hooks, among many others.
6. For a comprehensive overview of largely parallel courses of narrative studies and ethnic and postcolonial literature, as well as notable attempts (both successful and flawed) to bridge between them, see Kim, "Introduction."
7. Phelan, "Narrative Ethics."
8. Ibid.
9. For an example of the popular argument in favor of empathy as a salutary effect of fiction reading, see Pinker, *The Better Angels of Our Nature*. Recent scientific studies, widely reported in the popular press, also seem to corroborate the assumption that reading literary fiction, in particular, cultivates a sensitivity to the complexities of others' minds. See Chiaet, "Novel Finding."
10. Nussbaum, *Cultivating Humanity*, 10–11.
11. Keen, *Empathy and the Novel*, xiv.
12. Ibid., 28–34.
13. The findings of this study suggest that rather than inviting readers to freely enter into the minds of others, free indirect discourse can have the opposite

effect, dramatizing the fallacy of assuming one can ever truly know another's thoughts or see the world from his or her perspective. Fletcher and Monterosso, "The Science of Free-Indirect Discourse."

14. Hammond and Kim, "Introduction," 7. It is worth noting that the definitions of "sympathy" and "empathy" have shifted from the nineteenth to the twenty-first century; I use the terms here in their contemporary senses.

15. Cited in Palumbo-Liu, *The Deliverance of Others*, 6.

16. Following Derrida, this singularity derives from the fact of mortality, since in the moment of one's death no one else can be substituted in one's place: "It is from the site of death as the place of my irreplaceability, that is, of my singularity, that I feel called to responsibility. In this sense only a mortal can be responsible." *The Gift of Death*, 41.

17. A foundational source for many subsequent theorists of poststructuralist ethics, the moral philosophy of Emmanuel Levinas describes the encounter with the other whose difference is the source of an absolute and a priori ethical responsibility: "Responsibility for the Other, for the naked face of the first individual to come along . . . goes beyond what I may or may not have done to the Other or whatever acts I may or may not have committed, as if I were devoted to the other man before being devoted to myself. Or more exactly, as if I had to answer for the other's death even before *being*." *The Levinas Reader*, 83.

18. Hale situates the aesthetic theories of "new ethicists" in relation to an earlier set of claims in the Anglo-American tradition about the ethical value of reading as cultivating "social emotions" toward others, often through feelings like sympathy and empathy. Among their ranks, she numbers scholars such as J. Hillis Miller, Gayatri Spivak, Judith Butler, Derek Attridge, Geoffrey Galt Harpham, and Michael André Bernstein. In light of poststructuralist critiques of knowledge as an instrument of power, she argues, the new ethicists retain the idea that literature might cultivate emotions that connect us to one another, while remaining aware that the otherness we encounter in and through fiction remains fundamentally unknowable. Hale, "Aesthetics and the New Ethics," 899. See also Hale, "Fiction as Restriction."

19. Hale, "Aesthetics and the New Ethics," 900.

20. Ibid., 901.

21. Newton, *Narrative Ethics*, 11.

22. Ibid., 57.

23. Morrison, *Beloved*, 173. Subsequent page numbers for this work appear in the text.

24. Kim, *Critiquing Postmodernism*, 2.

25. Ibid., 4.

26. Derrida, *The Gift of Death*, 82.

27. Attridge, *J. M. Coetzee & the Ethics of Reading*, 11. Emphasis mine.

28. Palumbo-Liu, *The Deliverance of Others*.

29. Black, *Fiction across Borders*, 3.

30. Ibid., 32.

31. Palumbo-Liu, *The Deliverance of Others*, 1.

32. Freud, "The Uncanny."

33. Gordon, *Ghostly Matters*, 8. For a similar analysis of the unspeakable presences within American social worlds, see Holland, *Raising the Dead*.

34. Derrida, *Specters of Marx*, 10.

35. Ibid., 26.

36. Su, *Ethics and Nostalgia in the Contemporary Novel*, 46–47.

37. Cited in ibid., 43.

38. Palumbo-Liu, *The Deliverance of Others*, 1.

39. Hale, "Aesthetics and the New Ethics," 901.

40. Roy, *The God of Small Things*, 208. Subsequent page numbers for this work appear in the text.

41. Levine, *Forms*.

42. For an account of how readers' previously established expectations influence their practices of reading, see Rabinowitz, *Before Reading*.

43. Black, *Fiction across Borders*, 31.

44. DeLillo, *Falling Man*, 46.

45. The entirety of the poststructuralist turn in postcolonial studies can be seen in such terms, although, as I have suggested, I see much value in its characteristic embrace of difference. For a more recent defense of literary texts that resist interpretation or translation, respectively, see Abbott, *Real Mysteries*; Apter, *Against World Literature*.

46. For a representative example of the debate and its parties, see Damrosch and Spivak, "Comparative Literature/World Literature."

1. Figures of Estrangement

1. Devi, "Pterodactyl, Puran Sahay, and Pirtha," 97. Subsequent page numbers for this work appear in the text.

2. For an analysis of the politics of knowledge production in *Beloved*, see Goldman, "'I Made the Ink.'"

3. Morrison, *Beloved*, 202. Subsequent page numbers for this work appear in the text.

4. Readings of *Beloved* through the lens of trauma theory offer a powerful account of the novel's depiction of memory and its costs; see, for instance, Morgenstern, "Mother's Milk and Sister's Blood."

5. As James Phelan puts it, "The interpretive maneuver most widely practiced by contemporary critics can be summarized in a two-word slogan: 'Always thematize!'" *Reading People, Reading Plots*, 27.

6. Devi, "The Author in Conversation," xi.

7. Morrison, "The Site of Memory," 193.

8. Aldama, *Postethnic Narrative Criticism*, 7.

9. Inverting the assumption that science fiction is to be read as a departure from the norms of realist representation, Chu, in *Do Metaphors Dream of Literal Sleep?*, contends that inasmuch as all acts of literary representation are to some extent estranging, they all engage, to various degrees, in the practices of science fiction. For a similar argument framed in terms of fantasy, rather than science fiction, see Hume, *Fantasy and Mimesis*.

10. Chu, *Do Metaphors Dream of Literal Sleep?*, 7.

11. Alber, "Unnatural Spaces and Narrative Worlds."

12. Tapia, *American Pietàs*, 69–70.

13. Alber, "Unnatural Spaces and Narrative Worlds," 48.

14. Quoted in Chu, *Do Metaphors Dream of Literal Sleep?*, 10.

15. Faris notably includes *Beloved* in her foundational study of the genre, *Ordinary Enchantments*. For other magical realist readings of the novel, see Anderson, *Spectrality in the Novels of Toni Morrison*; Huber, "Ethical Magic."

16. Faris, *Ordinary Enchantments*, 1.

17. "The approach to the imaginary locality, or localized daydream, practiced by the genre of SF is a supposedly factual one. . . . Thus SF takes off from a fictional ('literary') hypothesis and develops it with extrapolating and totalizing ('scientific') rigor." Suvin, "On the Poetics of the Science Fiction Genre," 374.

18. Abbott, *Real Mysteries*, 17.

19. Ibid., 9.

20. Romagnolo, *Opening Acts*, 75.

21. Spivak, "Translator's Preface," xxiii.

22. As Jennifer Wenzel has observed, Spivak's framing of the stories amplifies the warnings they provide about the dangers of uninformed or reductive reading, "function[ing] at times as preemptive (presumptive?) scoldings for readings gone wrong." Wenzel, "Grim Fairy Tales," 232.

23. Devi, "The Author in Conversation," xi.

24. Ibid.

25. Wenzel, "Grim Fairy Tales," 230.

26. Lazarus, "Epilogue"; Ratti, *The Postsecular Imagination*.

27. See, for example, Weinstein, *What Else But Love?*; Moreland, "'He Wants to Put His Story Next to Hers'"; Woidat, "Talking Back to Schoolteacher."

28. See, for instance, Rushdy, "'Rememory'"; Rody, "Toni Morrison's *Beloved*"; Perez, "The Debt of Memory."

29. See, for instance, Holmes, "'This Is Flesh I'm Talking about Here'"; Barnett, "Figurations of Rape and the Supernatural in *Beloved*."

30. For more on the reading practices inspired by Oprah's Book Club, see Chabot Davis, "Oprah's Book Club and the Politics of Cross-Racial Empathy."

2. Telling the Traumas of History

1. These references are so common that they seem almost obligatory in descriptions of trauma: see, for example, Caruth, "Trauma and Experience," 4; LaCapra, *Writing History, Writing Trauma*, 14; Laub, "Truth and Testimony," 63; Cvetkovich, *An Archive of Feelings*, 6.

2. Caruth, "Trauma and Experience," 4–5.

3. Gregg and Seigworth, "An Inventory of Shimmers," 7.

4. Cvetkovich, *An Archive of Feelings*, 12.

5. For a fuller account of Ts'eh's mythic resonances, see Nelson and Nelson, "Shifting Patterns, Changing Stories."

6. Both Scott Richard Lyons and Sean Kicummah Teuton have recently explored this dynamic at length. Lyons, in *X-Marks*, is critical of "culture cops" (xii) whose engagements with Native culture reify the supposed binary between traditionalism and acculturation. In a similar vein, Teuton, in *Red Land, Red Power*, resists rigid formulations of Native American identity, drawing instead on a flexible and dynamic understanding of experience and identity to ground and evaluate claims to knowledge.

7. Wald, "The Culture of 'Internal Colonialism,'" 26.

8. Silko, *Ceremony*, 8. Subsequent page numbers for this work appear in the text.

9. Rand, "Surviving What Haunts You," 24.

10. Roy, *The God of Small Things*, 12. Subsequent page numbers for this work appear in the text.

11. Needham, "'The Small Voice of History,'" 372.

12. Ahmad, "Reading Arundhati Roy Politically," 104. Ahmad is right to recognize that the turn toward the personal often works hand in glove with the exotifying tendencies in postcolonial works marketed to Western readerships. However, for reasons I hope will become clear, I see the novel's depiction of the intimate terrains of sexuality and the family as constitutive of, rather than antithetical to, its political critique.

13. Judith Herman, for instance, offers an evocative description of the traumatic narrative as "a series of still snapshots or a silent movie; the role of therapy is to provide the music and the words." *Trauma and Recovery*, 175.

14. In contrast to a writer like Devi, whose fiction is written in Bengali and translated into English, Roy wrote *The God of Small Things* originally in English, a decision with especially complex cultural and political implications in the Indian context. By choosing to write in English, Roy addresses her fiction preferentially to a specific segment of the Indian population—middle- and upper-class readers likely to have received an English-medium education—and also facilitates its circulation abroad.

15. The defining features of traumatic literary narrative, derived from clinical contexts, have been codified in the work of literary scholars including, most prominently, Cathy Caruth. While, as Joshua Pederson, in "Speak, Trauma," suggests, certain elements of her model bear revision in light of current developments in psychological research, its substance remains largely unchallenged.

16. Rabinowitz, *Before Reading*, 43–44.

17. Phelan, *Narrative as Rhetoric.*

18. Herman, *Trauma and Recovery*, 140.

19. Ibid.

20. Caruth, "Trauma and Experience," 10.

21. Ibid., 11.

22. Ibid.

23. Bell, "Circular Design in *Ceremony*," 24.

24. I myself have previously made a version of this argument, which I'd like to complicate here. Freed, "The Ethics of Identification." See also Bell, "Circular Design in *Ceremony*"; Brill de Ramírez, *Contemporary American Indian Literatures and the Oral Tradition.*

25. Teuton, *Red Land, Red Power*, 141.

26. On the question of shame and its (re)inscription in postcolonial literature, see Bewes, *The Event of Postcolonial Shame.*

27. Chavkin, "Introduction," 4.

28. Mitchell, "*Ceremony* as Ritual," 28.

29. Ruppert, "No Boundaries, Only Transitions," 176, 178.

30. Sequoya-Magdaleno, "Telling the *Différance*."

31. Allen, "Special Problems," 88.

32. LaCapra, *Writing History, Writing Trauma*, 212.

33. Ibid., 211.

34. Ibid., 187.

35. Silko herself, in interviews, has linked Tayo's trauma and healing to her own psychological state; nevertheless, distinguishing Silko's experience from her characters' remains essential to any critical analysis of the novel. Cohen, "Of Apricots, Orchids, and Wovoka."

3. Invisible Victims, Visible Absences

1. Amnesty International, *Disappearances and Political Killings*, 84.

2. Phelan, *Reading People, Reading Plots*, 2.

3. Diana Taylor characterizes the Madres' iconic protest movement as "a public and ritualistic display of mourning" and theorizes its performative dimension as a form of "'restored' or 'twice-behaved behavior,'" calling attention to the untimely quality of the Madres' rhetorical appeal. *Disappearing Acts*, 186.

4. Ondaatje, *Anil's Ghost*, Author's Note. Subsequent page numbers for this work appear in the text.

5. Su, *Ethics and Nostalgia in the Contemporary Novel*, 44.

6. Many scholars have noted the various ways in which the Enlightenment-based legal and philosophical underpinnings of human rights give rise to troubling assumptions and exclusions, so much so that, as Elizabeth Anker has observed, "it has become a near truism to say that human rights 'have only paradoxes to offer.'" *Fictions of Dignity*, 2.

7. Nelson, *Political Bodies*, 50.

8. Amnesty International, *Disappearances and Political Killings*, 84.

9. As Elaine Scarry suggests, physical pain both undermines the linguistic powers of the person experiencing it and creates uncertainty in the person to whom it is reported. The disappeared person who becomes a victim of torture is thus subjected to a double erasure: removed from public view and denied recognition as a bearer of rights through the act of extrajudicial detention, and removed again, by the experience of inexpressible pain, from participation in the public discourse. *The Body in Pain*, 4.

10. As James Dawes points out, the presence of onlookers may actually motivate and shape, rather than restrain, acts of violence, which in such instances take on the quality of public performances. *That the World May Know*, 169.

11. Taylor, *Disappearing Acts*, 10.

12. Ibid., 123.

13. Nelson, *Political Bodies*, 50.

14. Dawes, *That the World May Know*, 9.

15. Schaffer and Smith, *Human Rights and Narrated Lives*, 6. Although Schaffer and Smith focus on autobiographical narrative, the questions they pose are equally thought-provoking in the context of other forms of representation, both nonfictional and fictional.

16. The United States' involvement in the 1973 coup was still the subject of debate at the time of *Missing*'s release. Subsequently, the nature and degree of that involvement, which included covert actions to destabilize the Allende government and provide resources to its opponents, has become a matter of scholarly consensus corroborated by the ongoing release of formerly classified documents.

17. The film is fictional but "based on a true story," conforming closely with a nonfictional account written by Thomas Hauser, which was not widely read at the time of its initial publication in 1978. The movie's screenplay is by Costa-Gavras and Donald E. Stewart.

18. *Missing*, dir. Costa-Gavras.

19. Quoted in Crowdus and Rubenstein, "The Missing Dossier," 32.

20. The final words of this address to the prisoners are not subtitled, and the translation is mine.

21. Dorfman, "Fictionalizing the Truth in Latin America," 796.

22. Ibid.

23. During an intense period of fighting in Sri Lanka between 1987 and 1990, Amnesty International, *Disappearances and Political Killings*, 28, estimates that

tens of thousands of people were victims of disappearance or extrajudicial killing. In 2009, the Sri Lankan government declared victory over the Tamil separatists, and emergency laws were lifted in 2010. As of this writing, however, the
political situation in the country remains uncertain, and the practices of disappearance, torture, and extrajudicial killing persist. Amnesty International, "Sri
Lanka's Shameful Record."

24. Ratti, "Michael Ondaatje's *Anil's Ghost* and the Aestheticization of Human
Rights," 123–24.

25. For a persuasive account of the novel through the lens of postcolonial de-
tective fiction, which strategically undermines the conventions of the form, see
Siddiqi, *Anxieties of Empire and the Fiction of Intrigue*. See also Chakravorty, "The
Dead That Haunt *Anil's Ghost*."

26. LeClair, "The Sri Lankan Patients," 32; Ismail, "A Flippant Gesture Towards Sri Lanka," 28.

27. Ismail, *Abiding by Sri Lanka*, 16.

28. Ibid., 17.

29. Ibid., 17–18.

30. Chakravorty makes a similar observation about the novel's inability to
render victims of the Sri Lankan conflict as particular individuals, which she links
to the stereotypical association between death and the postcolony. "The Dead
That Haunt *Anil's Ghost*," 542.

31. McClennen and Slaughter, "Introducing Human Rights and Literary
Forms," 10.

32. Ibid.

33. Among its widely recognized shortcomings, the logic of human rights
is grounded in the Western Enlightenment tradition and the construct of legal
personhood (see Slaughter, *Human Rights, Inc.*), predicated on the conceit of
bodily integrity (see Anker, *Fictions of Dignity*), or, most troublingly, rendered
vulnerable by its very prevalence to appropriation and abuse (see Anker, *Fictions
of Dignity* and Dawes, *That the World May Know*).

34. Anker, *Fictions of Dignity*, 35.

4. Haunting Futures and the Dystopian Imagination

1. DeLillo, *Falling Man*, 191. Subsequent page numbers for this work appear
in the text.

2. Armah, *Beautyful Ones*, 10. Subsequent page numbers for this work appear in the text.

3. In a convincing reading of Armah's novel, John Lutz uses the framework
of Marxist commodity fetishism to illuminate "the implicit connection between the 'clean life' lived within the gleam and the miserable, abject one lived
among mountains of waste and excrement," both of which are the products of

"a monolithic system of commodity production and exchange." "Pessimism, Autonomy, and Commodity Fetishism," 103–4.

4. Esty, "Excremental Postcolonialism," 32.

5. Kibera, "Pessimism and the African Novelist," 71.

6. Ibid. Fellow Ghanaian writer Ama Ata Aidoo has been another prominent critic of *Beautyful Ones*, and her own short story collection, *No Sweetness Here*, published in 1970, can be read as a response to it.

7. Corrigan, "Don DeLillo's 'Falling Man.'"

8. Kakutani, "A Man, a Woman and a Day of Terror," 2.

9. Corrigan, "Don DeLillo's 'Falling Man.'"

10. Kibera, "Pessimism and the African Novelist," 70.

11. Moylan, *Scraps of the Untainted Sky*, 147.

12. Booker, *The Dystopian Impulse in Modern Literature*, 19.

13. Wright, "'Dystropia' in the African Novel," 30.

14. Esty, "Excremental Postcolonialism," 33. Esty's reading of the role of excrement in *Beautyful Ones* foregrounds the self-reproach that scatological imagery encodes, pointing to the complicity of intellectuals such as the novel's protagonist—and its author—in the flawed social system they critique.

15. Versluys, *Out of the Blue*, 20. For a more inclusive treatment of DeLillo's engagement with contemporary American culture and society, see Osteen, *American Magic and Dread*.

16. Darko Suvin's foundational definition of science fiction also describes the effect sought by dystopian literature written in other genres, which "estranges the author's and reader's own empirical environment" in service of an alternative vision. "Radical Rhapsody and Romantic Recoil in the Age of Anticipation," 255.

17. Moylan, *Scraps of the Untainted Sky*, 154.

18. Ibid., 156–57.

19. Jameson, *Archaeologies of the Future*, xv.

20. Ibid., xiii.

21. Ibid., xv.

22. In his provocative article, Glen Retief identifies the powerful homoerotic undercurrents that are also at work in this scene. Although Teacher succeeds in "mentor[ing] the man back to conventional, familial heterosexuality," the scene nevertheless contains "a veritable plethora of signs pointing away from married, domestic heterosexuality in the direction of the homoerotic." "Homoeroticism and the Failure of African Nationalism," 67.

23. Lutz, "Pessimism, Autonomy, and Commodity Fetishism," 104.

24. Spencer, "'This Zone of Occult Instability,'" 82–83.

25. Lazarus, *Resistance in Postcolonial African Fiction*, 78.

26. Ibid., 73.

27. Wenzel, "Remembering the Past's Future."

28. Kaledzi, "Outrage in Ghana."

29. Rabinowitz, "'Betraying the Sender,'" 205.

30. See, for instance, Rodin, *The Resilience Dividend*.

Conclusion

1. Harris, *What's So Funny about Science?*

2. Kim, *Critiquing Postmodernism*, 1.

3. Damrosch, *What Is World Literature?*; Casanova, *The World Republic of Letters*; Moretti, *Distant Reading*; Walkowitz, *Cosmopolitan Style*.

4. Damrosch, *What Is World Literature?*, 4.

5. Moretti, *Graphs, Maps, Trees*.

6. See Damrosch and Spivak, "Comparative Literature/World Literature," in which Damrosch persuasively traces the links between the study of world literature in translation and the democratization of the U.S. academy in the 1950s and 1960s.

7. Apter, *Against World Literature*, 20.

8. Ibid., 31.

9. Damrosch and Spivak, "Comparative Literature/World Literature," 474.

10. Ngai, *Ugly Feelings*, 3. Ngai argues that lesser passions like envy and irritation, in particular, can be read as allegories "for an autonomous or bourgeois art's increasingly resigned and pessimistic understanding of its *own* relationship to political action" (ibid.)—in other words, these affects reflect fiction's relationship to reality.

11. Appiah, *Cosmopolitanism*.

12. Massumi, *Politics of Affect*, ix.

13. Robbins, *Feeling Global*, 6.

Bibliography

Abbott, H. Porter. *Real Mysteries: Narrative and the Unknowable*. Columbus: Ohio State University Press, 2013.

Achebe, Chinua. *Things Fall Apart*. Expanded ed. with notes. African Writers Series. Oxford: Heinemann Educational, 1996.

Adichie, Chimamanda Ngozi. *Americanah: A Novel*. New York: Knopf, 2013.

Ahmad, Aijaz. "Reading Arundhati Roy Politically." *Frontline*, August 8, 1997, 103–8.

Aidoo, Ama Ata. *No Sweetness Here*. London: Longman, 1970.

Alber, Jan. "Unnatural Spaces and Narrative Worlds." In *A Poetics of Unnatural Narrative*, edited by Henrik Skov Nielsen, Brian Richardson, and Jan Alber, 45–66. Columbus: Ohio State University Press, 2013.

Aldama, Frederick Luis. *Postethnic Narrative Criticism: Magicorealism in Oscar "Zeta" Acosta, Ana Castillo, Julie Dash, Hanif Kureishi, and Salman Rushdie*. Austin: University of Texas Press, 2003.

Allen, Paula Gunn. "Special Problems in Teaching Leslie Marmon Silko's *Ceremony*." In *Leslie Marmon Silko's "Ceremony": A Casebook*, edited by Allan Richard Chavkin, 83–90. Oxford: Oxford University Press, 2002.

Amnesty International. *Disappearances and Political Killings: Human Rights Crisis of the 1990s: A Manual for Action*. Amsterdam: Amnesty International, 1994.

———. "Sri Lanka's Shameful Record on Detention Without Trial," March 13, 2012. http://www.amnesty.org/en/for-media/press-releases/sri-lanka-s-shameful-record-detention-without-trial-2012-03-13.

Anderson, Melanie R. *Spectrality in the Novels of Toni Morrison*. Knoxville: University of Tennessee Press, 2013.

Anker, Elizabeth S. *Fictions of Dignity: Embodying Human Rights in World Literature*. Ithaca: Cornell University Press, 2012.

Appiah, Kwame Anthony. *Cosmopolitanism: Ethics in a World of Strangers.* New York: Norton, 2007.

Apter, Emily. *Against World Literature: On the Politics of Untranslatability.* New York: Verso, 2013.

Armah, Ayi Kwei. *The Beautyful Ones Are Not Yet Born.* African Writers Series. London: Heinemann, 1988.

Attridge, Derek. *J. M. Coetzee and the Ethics of Reading: Literature in the Event.* Chicago: University of Chicago Press, 2004.

Atwood, Margaret. *The Handmaid's Tale.* Boston: Houghton Mifflin Harcourt, 1986.

Barnett, Pamela E. "Figurations of Rape and the Supernatural in *Beloved.*" *PMLA* 112, no. 3 (1997): 418–27.

Bell, Robert C. "Circular Design in *Ceremony.*" In *Leslie Marmon Silko's "Ceremony": A Casebook,* edited by Allan Richard Chavkin, 23–39. Oxford: Oxford University Press, 2002.

Bewes, Timothy. *The Event of Postcolonial Shame.* Princeton, NJ: Princeton University Press, 2010.

Black, Shameem. *Fiction across Borders: Imagining the Lives of Others in Late Twentieth-Century Novels.* New York: Columbia University Press, 2010.

Booker, M. Keith. *The Dystopian Impulse in Modern Literature: Fiction as Social Criticism.* Westport: Greenwood Press, 1994.

Brill de Ramírez, Susan Berry. *Contemporary American Indian Literatures and the Oral Tradition.* Tucson: University of Arizona Press, 1999.

Brogan, Kathleen. *Cultural Haunting: Ghosts and Ethnicity in Recent American Literature.* Charlottesville: University Press of Virginia, 1998.

Caruth, Cathy. "Trauma and Experience: Introduction." In *Trauma: Explorations in Memory,* edited by Cathy Caruth, 3–12. Baltimore: Johns Hopkins University Press, 1995.

Casanova, Pascale. *The World Republic of Letters.* Cambridge, MA: Harvard University Press, 2004.

Chabot Davis, Kimberly. "Oprah's Book Club and the Politics of Cross-Racial Empathy." *International Journal of Cultural Studies* 7, no. 4 (2004): 399–419.

Chakravorty, Mrinalini. "The Dead That Haunt *Anil's Ghost*: Subaltern Difference and Postcolonial Melancholia." *PMLA* 128, no. 3 (2013): 542–58.

Chavkin, Allan Richard. "Introduction." In *Leslie Marmon Silko's "Ceremony": A Casebook,* edited by Allan Richard Chavkin, 3–15. Oxford: Oxford University Press, 2002.

Chiaet, Julianne. "Novel Finding: Reading Literary Fiction Improves Empathy." *Scientific American,* October 4, 2013. https://www.scientificamerican.com/article/novel-finding-reading-literary-fiction-improves-empathy/.

Chu, Seo-Young. *Do Metaphors Dream of Literal Sleep? A Science-Fictional Theory of Representation*. Cambridge, MA: Harvard University Press, 2010.

Cohen, Robin. "Of Apricots, Orchids, and Wovoka: An Interview with Leslie Marmon Silko." In *Leslie Marmon Silko's "Ceremony": A Casebook*, edited by Allan Richard Chavkin, 257–63. Oxford: Oxford University Press, 2002.

Corrigan, Maureen. "Don DeLillo's 'Falling Man.'" *Fresh Air*, May 16, 2007. http://www.npr.org/templates/story/story.php?storyId=10207877.

Crowdus, Gary, and Lenny Rubenstein. "The Missing Dossier." *Cineaste* 12 (1982): 30–38.

Cvetkovich, Ann. *An Archive of Feelings: Trauma, Sexuality, and Lesbian Public Cultures*. Durham, NC: Duke University Press, 2003.

Damrosch, David. *What Is World Literature?* Princeton, NJ: Princeton University Press, 2003.

Damrosch, David, and Gayatri Chakravorty Spivak. "Comparative Literature/World Literature: A Discussion with Gayatri Chakravorty Spivak and David Damrosch." *Comparative Literature Studies* 48, no. 4 (2011): 455–85.

Dangarembga, Tsitsi. *Nervous Conditions: A Novel*. New York: Seal Press, 2004.

Dawes, James. *That the World May Know: Bearing Witness to Atrocity*. Cambridge, MA: Harvard University Press, 2007.

DeLillo, Don. *Falling Man: A Novel*. New York: Scribner, 2007.

Derrida, Jacques. *The Gift of Death*. Religion and Postmodernism. Chicago: University of Chicago Press, 1995.

——. *Specters of Marx: The State of the Debt, the Work of Mourning, and the New International*. New York: Routledge, 1994.

Devi, Mahasweta. "The Author in Conversation." In *Imaginary Maps: Three Stories*, edited by Gayatri Chakravorty Spivak, ix–xxii. New York: Routledge, 1995.

——. "Pterodactyl, Puran Sahay, and Pirtha." In *Imaginary Maps: Three Stories*, translated by Gayatri Chakravorty Spivak, 95–196. New York: Routledge, 1995.

Dorfman, Ariel. "Fictionalizing the Truth in Latin America." *Nation*, June 25, 1983, 794–86.

Esty, Joshua D. "Excremental Postcolonialism." *Contemporary Literature* 40 (1999): 22–59.

Eugenides, Jeffrey. *Middlesex: A Novel*. New York: Picador, 2002.

Faris, Wendy B. *Ordinary Enchantments*. Nashville: Vanderbilt University Press, 2004.

Fletcher, Angus, and John Monterosso. "The Science of Free-Indirect Discourse: An Alternate Cognitive Effect." *Narrative* 24, no. 1 (2016): 82–103.

Freed, Joanne Lipson. "The Ethics of Identification: The Global Circulation of Traumatic Narrative in Silko's *Ceremony* and Roy's *The God of Small Things*." *Comparative Literature Studies* 48, no. 2 (2011): 219–40.

Freud, Sigmund. "The Uncanny." In *The Standard Edition of the Complete Psychological Works of Sigmund Freud*, edited by James Strachey, 17:217–56. London: Hogarth Press, 1953.

Gates, Henry Louis, Jr. *The Signifying Monkey: A Theory of Afro-American Literary Criticism*. New York: Oxford University Press, 1988.

Goldman, Anne E. "'I Made the Ink': (Literary) Production and Reproduction in *Dessa Rose* and *Beloved*." *Feminist Studies* 16 (1990): 313–30.

Gordon, Avery. *Ghostly Matters: Haunting and the Sociological Imagination*. Minneapolis: University of Minnesota Press, 1997.

Gregg, Melissa, and Gregory J. Seigworth. "An Inventory of Shimmers." In *The Affect Theory Reader*, edited by Melissa Gregg and Gregory J. Seigworth, 1–25. Durham, NC: Duke University Press, 2010.

Hale, Dorothy J. "Aesthetics and the New Ethics: Theorizing the Novel in the Twenty-First Century." *PMLA* 124, no. 3 (2009): 896–905.

——. "Fiction as Restriction: Self-Binding in New Ethical Theories of the Novel." *Narrative* 15, no. 2 (2007): 187–206.

Hall, Stuart. *Representation: Cultural Representations and Signifying Practices*. Thousand Oaks, CA: Sage, 1997.

Hammond, Meghan Marie, and Sue J. Kim. "Introduction." In *Rethinking Empathy through Literature*, edited by Meghan Marie Hammond and Sue J. Kim, 1–18. New York: Routledge, 2014.

Harris, Sidney. *What's So Funny about Science? Cartoons from American Scientist*. Los Altos, CA: William Kaufmann, 1977.

Hemingway, Ernest. *A Farewell to Arms*. New York: Scribner, 1957.

Herman, Judith Lewis. *Trauma and Recovery*. New York: Basic Books, 1992.

Holland, Sharon Patricia. *Raising the Dead: Readings of Death and (Black) Subjectivity*. Durham, NC: Duke University Press, 2000.

Holmes, Kristine. "'This Is Flesh I'm Talking about Here': Embodiment in Toni Morrison's *Beloved* and Sherley Anne Williams' *Dessa Rose*." *Lit: Literature Interpretation Theory* 6, nos. 1–2 (1995): 133–48.

hooks, bell. *Black Looks: Race and Representation*. Boston: South End Press, 1992.

Huber, Irmtraud. "Ethical Magic: Traumatic Magic Realism in Toni Morrison's *Beloved*." *Zeitschrift für Anglistik und Amerikanistik: A Quarterly of Language, Literature and Culture* 58, no. 4 (2010): 367–79.

Hume, Kathryn. *Fantasy and Mimesis: Responses to Reality in Western Literature*. New York: Methuen, 1984.

Ismail, Qadri. *Abiding by Sri Lanka: On Peace, Place, and Postcoloniality*. Minneapolis: University of Minnesota Press, 2005.

——. "A Flippant Gesture Towards Sri Lanka: A Review of Michael Ondaatje's *Anil's Ghost*." *Pravada* 6, no. 9 (2000): 24–29.

Jameson, Fredric. *Archaeologies of the Future: The Desire Called Utopia and Other Science Fictions*. New York: Verso, 2005.

Jones, Gayl. *Corregidora*. New York: Random House, 1975.

Kakutani, Michiko. "A Man, a Woman and a Day of Terror." *New York Times*, May 9, 2007.

Kaledzi, Isaac. "Outrage in Ghana over Guantanamo Detainees." *DW. COM*, January 7, 2106. http://www.dw.com/en/outrage-in-ghana-over-guantanamo-detainees/a-18966198.

Keen, Suzanne. *Empathy and the Novel*. Oxford: Oxford University Press, 2007.

Kibera, Leonard. "Pessimism and the African Novelist: Ayi Kwei Armah's *The Beautyful Ones Are Not Yet Born*." *Journal of Commonwealth Literature* 14, no. 1 (1979): 64–72.

Kim, Sue J. *Critiquing Postmodernism in Contemporary Discourses of Race*. New York: Palgrave, 2009.

——. "Introduction." In *Decolonizing Narrative Theory*, special issue, *Journal of Narrative Theory* 42, no. 3 (2013): 233–47.

LaCapra, Dominick. *Writing History, Writing Trauma*. Baltimore: Johns Hopkins University Press, 2001.

Laub, Dori. "Truth and Testimony: The Process and the Struggle." In *Trauma: Explorations in Memory*, edited by Cathy Caruth, 61–75. Baltimore: Johns Hopkins University Press, 1995.

Lazarus, Neil. "Epilogue: The Pterodactyl of History?" *Textual Practice* 27, no. 3 (May 2013): 523–36.

——. *Resistance in Postcolonial African Fiction*. New Haven: Yale University Press, 1990.

LeClair, Tom. "The Sri Lankan Patients." *Nation*, June 19, 2000, 31–33.

Levinas, Emmanuel. *The Levinas Reader*. Edited by Sean Hand. Hoboken: Wiley-Blackwell, 2001.

Levine, Caroline. *Forms: Whole, Rhythm, Hierarchy, Network*. Princeton, NJ: Princeton University Press, 2015.

Lutz, John. "Pessimism, Autonomy, and Commodity Fetishism in Ayi Kwei Armah's *The Beautyful Ones Are Not Yet Born*." *Research in African Literatures* 34, no. 2 (2003): 94–111.

Lyons, Scott Richard. *X-Marks: Native Signatures of Assent*. Minneapolis: University of Minnesota Press, 2010.

Massumi, Brian. *Politics of Affect*. New York: Wiley, 2015.

McClennen, Sophia A., and Joseph R. Slaughter. "Introducing Human Rights and Literary Forms; or, The Vehicles and Vocabularies of Human Rights." *Comparative Literature Studies* 46, no. 1 (2009): 1–19.

Missing. Directed by Costa-Gavras. 1982. Universal City, CA: Universal Studios Home Entertainment, 2004. DVD.

Mitchell, Carol. "*Ceremony* as Ritual." *American Indian Quarterly* 5, no. 1 (1979): 27–35.

Moreland, Richard C. "'He Wants to Put His Story Next to Hers': Putting Twain's Story Next to Hers in Morrison's *Beloved*." *MFS: Modern Fiction Studies* 39, nos. 3–4 (1993): 501–25.

Moretti, Franco. *Distant Reading*. New York: Verso, 2013.

———. *Graphs, Maps, Trees: Abstract Models for a Literary History*. New York: Verso, 2005.

Morgenstern, Naomi. "Mother's Milk and Sister's Blood: Trauma and the Neoslave Narrative." *Differences: A Journal of Feminist Cultural Studies* 8, no. 2 (1996): 101–26.

Morrison, Toni. *Beloved: A Novel*. New York: Plume-Penguin, 1988.

———. *The Bluest Eye*. New York: Knopf, 1993.

———. "The Site of Memory." In *Inventing the Truth: The Art and Craft of Memoir*, edited by Russell Baker and William Knowlton Zinsser, 183–200. New York: Harcourt, 1998.

Moylan, Tom. *Scraps of the Untainted Sky: Science Fiction, Utopia, Dystopia*. Boulder: Westview Press, 2000.

Needham, Anuradha Dingwaney. "'The Small Voice of History' in Arundhati Roy's *The God of Small Things*." *Interventions: International Journal of Postcolonial Studies* 7, no. 3 (2005): 369–91.

Nelson, Alice. *Political Bodies: Gender, History, and the Struggle for Narrative Power in Recent Chilean Literature*. Lewisburg: Bucknell University Press, 2002.

Nelson, Elizabeth Hoffman, and Malcolm A. Nelson. "Shifting Patterns, Changing Stories: Leslie Marmon Silko's Yellow Women." In *Leslie Marmon Silko: A Collection of Critical Essays*, edited by Louise K. Barnett and James L. Thorson, 121–34. Albuquerque: University of New Mexico Press, 2001.

Newton, Adam Zachary. *Narrative Ethics*. Cambridge, MA: Harvard University Press, 2009.

Ngai, Sianne. *Ugly Feelings*. Cambridge, MA: Harvard University Press, 2005.

Nussbaum, Martha Craven. *Cultivating Humanity: A Classical Defense of Reform in Liberal Education*. Cambridge, MA: Harvard University Press, 1998.

Ondaatje, Michael. *Anil's Ghost*. New York: Random House, 2001.

Osteen, Mark. *American Magic and Dread: Don DeLillo's Dialogue with Culture*. Philadelphia: University of Pennsylvania Press, 2000.

Palumbo-Liu, David. *The Deliverance of Others: Reading Literature in a Global Age*. Durham, NC: Duke University Press, 2012.

Pederson, Joshua. "Speak, Trauma: Toward a Revised Understanding of Literary Trauma Theory." *Narrative* 22, no. 3 (2014): 333–53.

Perez, Richard. "The Debt of Memory: Reparations, Imagination, and History in Toni Morrison's *Beloved*." *WSQ: Women's Studies Quarterly* 42, nos. 1–2 (2014): 190–98.

Phelan, James. *Narrative as Rhetoric: Technique, Audiences, Ethics, Ideology*. Columbus: Ohio State University Press, 1996.

———. "Narrative Ethics." *The Living Handbook of Narratology*. Hamburg University, November 21, 2013. http://www.lhn.uni-hamburg.de/.

———. *Reading People, Reading Plots: Character, Progression, and the Interpretation of Narrative*. Chicago: University of Chicago Press, 1989.

Pinker, Steven. *The Better Angels of Our Nature: Why Violence Has Declined*. New York: Viking, 2011.

Rabinowitz, Peter J. *Before Reading: Narrative Conventions and the Politics of Interpretation*. Columbus: Ohio State University Press, 1998.

———. "'Betraying the Sender': The Rhetoric and Ethics of Fragile Texts." *Narrative* 2, no. 3 (1994): 201–13.

Rand, Naomi R. "Surviving What Haunts You: The Art of Invisibility in *Ceremony*, *The Ghost Writer*, and *Beloved*." *MELUS* 20, no. 3 (1995): 21–32.

Ratti, Manav. "Michael Ondaatje's *Anil's Ghost* and the Aestheticization of Human Rights." *ARIEL: A Review of International English Literature* 35, nos. 1–2 (2004): 121–39.

———. *The Postsecular Imagination: Postcolonialism, Religion, and Literature*. New York: Routledge, 2013.

Resnick, Mike. *Kirinyaga*. New York: Random House, 2009.

Retief, Glen. "Homoeroticism and the Failure of African Nationalism in Ayi Kwei Armah's *The Beautyful Ones*." *Research in African Literatures* 40, no. 3 (2009): 62–73.

Robbins, Bruce. *Feeling Global: Internationalism in Distress*. New York: New York University Press, 1999.

Rodin, Judith. *The Resilience Dividend: Managing Disruption, Avoiding Disaster, and Growing Stronger in an Unpredictable World*. New York: PublicAffairs, 2014.

Rody, Caroline. "Toni Morrison's *Beloved*: History, 'Rememory,' and a 'Clamor for a Kiss.'" *American Literary History* 7, no. 1995 (1995): 92–119.

Romagnolo, Catherine. *Opening Acts: Narrative Beginnings in Twentieth-Century Feminist Fiction.* Lincoln: University of Nebraska Press, 2015.

Roy, Arundhati. *The God of Small Things.* New York: HarperCollins, 1998.

Ruppert, James. "No Boundaries, Only Transitions: *Ceremony.*" In *Leslie Marmon Silko's "Ceremony": A Casebook,* edited by Allan Richard Chavkin, 175–91. Oxford: Oxford University Press, 2002.

Rushdy, Ashraf H.A. "'Rememory': Primal Scenes and Constructions in Toni Morrison's Novels." *Contemporary Literature* 31 (1990): 300–323.

Said, Edward W. *Culture and Imperialism.* New York: Vintage Books, 1994.

Scarry, Elaine. *The Body in Pain: The Making and Unmaking of the World.* Oxford: Oxford University Press, 1985.

Schaffer, Kay, and Sidonie Smith. *Human Rights and Narrated Lives: The Ethics of Recognition.* New York: Palgrave, 2004.

Sequoya-Magdaleno, Jana. "Telling the *Différance*: Representations of Identity in the Discourse of Indianness." In *The Ethnic Canon: Histories, Institutions, and Interventions,* edited by David Palumbo-Liu, 88–116. Minneapolis: University of Minnesota Press, 1995.

Siddiqi, Yumna. *Anxieties of Empire and the Fiction of Intrigue.* New York: Columbia University Press, 2008.

Silko, Leslie Marmon. *Ceremony.* New York: Penguin, 1986.

Slaughter, Joseph R. *Human Rights, Inc.: The World Novel, Narrative Form, and International Law.* New York: Fordham University Press, 2007.

Spencer, Robert. "'This Zone of Occult Instability': The Utopian Promise of the African Novel in the Era of Decolonisation." *New Formations: A Journal of Culture/Theory/Politics* 47 (2002): 69–86.

Spivak, Gayatri Chakravorty. "Can the Subaltern Speak?" In *Marxism and the Interpretation of Culture,* edited by Cary Nelson and Lawrence Grossberg, 271–313. Champaign: University of Illinois Press, 1988.

———. "Translator's Preface." In *Imaginary Maps: Three Stories,* edited by Gayatri Chakravorty Spivak, xxiii–xxix. New York: Routledge, 1995.

Su, John J. *Ethics and Nostalgia in the Contemporary Novel.* Cambridge: Cambridge University Press, 2005.

Suvin, Darko. "On the Poetics of the Science Fiction Genre." *College English* 34, no. 1972 (1972): 372–82.

———. "Radical Rhapsody and Romantic Recoil in the Age of Anticipation: A Chapter in the History of SF." *Science Fiction Studies* 1, no. 4 (Autumn 1974): 255–69.

Tapia, Ruby C. *American Pietàs: Visions of Race, Death, and the Maternal.* Minneapolis: University of Minnesota Press, 2011.

Taylor, Diana. *Disappearing Acts: Spectacles of Gender and Nationalism in Argentina's "Dirty War."* Durham, NC: Duke University Press, 1997.

Teuton, Sean Kicummah. *Red Land, Red Power: Grounding Knowledge in the American Indian Novel*. Durham, NC: Duke University Press, 2008.

Versluys, Kristiaan. *Out of the Blue: September 11 and the Novel*. New York: Columbia University Press, 2009.

Wald, Alan. "The Culture of 'Internal Colonialism': A Marxist Perspective." *MELUS* 8, no. 3 (1981): 18–27.

Walkowitz, Rebecca L. *Cosmopolitan Style: Modernism beyond the Nation*. New York: Columbia University Press, 2006.

Weinstein, Philip M. *What Else But Love? The Ordeal of Race in Faulkner and Morrison*. New York: Columbia University Press, 1996.

Wenzel, Jennifer. "Grim Fairy Tales: Taking a Risk, Reading *Imaginary Maps*." In *Going Global: The Transnational Reception of Third World Women Writers*, edited by Amal Amireh and Lisa Suhair Majaj, 229–51. New York: Garland, 2000.

———. "Remembering the Past's Future: Anti-Imperialist Nostalgia and Some Versions of the Third World." *Cultural Critique* 62 (2006): 1–32.

Woidat, Caroline M. "Talking Back to Schoolteacher: Morrison's Confrontation with Hawthorne in *Beloved*." *MFS: Modern Fiction Studies* 39, nos. 3–4 (1993): 527–46.

Wright, Derek. "'Dystropia' in the African Novel: A Critique of Armah's Language in *The Beautyful Ones Are Not Yet Born*." *Commonwealth Novel in English* 5, no. 2 (1992): 26–38.

Index

neocolonialism, 137. *See also*
    imperialism
"new ethicists," 11, 180n18
Newton, Adam, 12
New York City, post–9/11, 33, 131–32,
    135, 137, 156–62
Ngai, Sianne, 175, 188n10
nihilism, 159, 163
Nkrumah, Kwame, 144, 148
noncommunication, 173
nonindigenous readers, 79, 86–88.
    See also cross-cultural reading;
    majoritarian readers
nonlinearity, 80, 84. *See also* cyclical
    structure; temporal progression
No Sweetness Here (Aidoo), 187n6
Nussbaum, Martha, 9

Ondaatje, Michael, 28. See also *Anil's
    Ghost*
ontological difference, 18–19, 30
openness: structural, 135, 150–51,
    164–66; to unseen possibilities, 25
    (*see also* futures)
Oprah's Book Club, 67
optimism, 136, 145
otherness, 11–17. *See also* difference
"otherness postmodernism," 15, 170

Palumbo-Liu, David, 16–17, 20
particularity, 95, 173–74; of individuals,
    103, 108–9, 112, 127–28
Pederson, Joshua, 184n15
personal, political and, 75, 78, 122,
    124–25, 183n12
perspective-taking, literary, 70–71, 79,
    88, 92, 95, 98. *See also* identification
pessimism, 137–38, 140–52, 155, 164
Phelan, James, 8, 181n5
Pinochet, Augusto, 32, 109, 113, 116
Plato, 154
political disappearance. *See*
    disappearance, political
political modernity, 125

politics: and ethics, 27–28 (*see also*
    ethical relations); and felt experience,
    71–72; and personal experiences, 78,
    122, 124–25, 183n12. *See also* resistant
    narratives; social and political
    critiques
positionality, 88
postcolonial studies, 6–8, 15–18, 28,
    67, 181n45, 183n12; affective turn,
    174–76; linguistic turn, 169–70, 174,
    176; poststructuralist turn, 181n45
poststructuralist ethics, 2, 180n17
poststructuralist theory, 11, 170, 181n45
power, differences in, 2–5, 16, 38, 93
progression, 18–21, 64, 108, 120–21
psychological trauma. *See* trauma
"Pterodactyl, Puran Sahay, and
    Pirtha" (Devi), 1–3, 18, 29, 31;
    communication with others,
    41, 54–55, 60–62; conclusions,
    interpretations, and circulation,
    53–54, 62–68; emotional engagement,
    66; encounters with difference,
    42, 59–62; English translation, 66,
    183n14; exorcism, 54–56, 59–62;
    haunting, 21–23, 35–42; limits of
    knowledge, 37–42, 45–46, 53–55,
    60; magical realism, 52; mimetic
    representation, 46–51, 63–64;
    postscript, 63–64; thematic reading,
    67; transformation, 25, 61–62
purity, 140, 153; racial and cultural,
    73–74

Rabinowitz, Peter, 81, 165
Rand, Naomi, 74
Ratti, Manav, 67, 122
realism, 36, 46, 64; in haunted fiction,
    23–24; mimetic illusion, 16, 23,
    31–32, 36 (*see also* mimesis). *See also*
    magical realism
"rememory," 42–43
repetition, 79, 84, 149, 152, 159–62, 164,
    166